HTML in easy steps

Chris Russell

In easy steps is an imprint of Computer Step
Southfield Road . Southam
Warwickshire CV33 OFB . England

Tel: 01926 817999 Fax: 01926 817005
http://www.computerstep.com

Notice of Liability

Every effort has been made to ensure that this book contains accurate and current information. However, Computer Step and the author shall not be liable for any loss or damage suffered by readers as a result of any information contained herein.

Trademarks

All trademarks are acknowledged as belonging to their respective companies.

Printed and bound in the United Kingdom

ISBN 1-874029-86-5

Contents

Chapter One

Introduction

This chapter introduces the concepts of the Internet and the World Wide Web and provides a basic introduction to the language of the web – HTML.

Covers

What is the Internet?

The Internet is a huge collection of computers sited around the world and connected together to form a huge network allowing information to be collated and shared by many millions of people.

The idea of the Net is not a new one, having been originally planned in the early 1960s by the American military as a way of preserving communications in the event of a nuclear war.

However, as time passed, the original network of a handful of computers in the United States expanded rapidly as universities and scientists realised it was a unique way of passing on shared knowledge and research work.

Through the 1970s and early 80s the popularity of the Internet grew exponentially as the educational establishment clamoured to sign up for the on-line experience and enterprising entrepreneurs realised there was great potential in selling Internet access into the home.

There is a general title on the Internet in this same series, called Internet UK in easy steps.

Having achieved massive success in the US the Net was to enjoy a second wind of popularity when the UK and Europe cottoned onto its potential in the mid 1980's. Even now, 60 years after its inception people are queuing up across the globe to get onto the Internet and find out what all of the fuss is about.

Estimates currently place the number of people worldwide with access to the Net in excess of 40 million and growing rapidly as business and home users realise the potential of this 'new' communications medium.

It has been described as the second greatest invention of the 20th century (after the TV) and is sure to become a rapidly increasing part of everyday life providing global communications and information sharing on an unprecedented scale.

How the Internet Works

It is a popular misconception that the Internet is a single entity with branches around the world.

In reality the Net is a huge collection of smaller networks connected together using special protocols and specialised computers called routers.

Each of the smaller networks is registered with these routers which contain huge lists of data which allow them to pass data easily between them. The system works in a similar way to the UK telephone system – imagine a situation where a phone user in Reading wants to make a call to a family in Hull.

For a more detailed history of the growth of the Internet visit http://www.davesite.com/webstation/net-history.shtml

The first stage of the operation involves picking up the phone and dialling the required number. The local telephone exchange (the router on the Internet) picks up the number dialled and decides whether it falls within its own jurisdiction or needs to be sent on long-distance lines. If it's a local call the exchange deals with it immediately. If not it consults its list of telephone exchanges around the country and sends the call to the nearest one.

In order to send data in a reliable way the Internet uses a special set of communication methods, or protocols. The most common is TCP/IP or Transmission Control Protocol. Using such methods means that data can be sent and received across the whole Internet without problems, irrespective of any specialised protocols that may be used within any particular area – it's rather like a Frenchman talking to a Chinese woman through an interpreter. Both use their own specific languages within their own areas but the interpreter allows them to communicate clearly without the chance for misunderstandings.

At face level the inner workings of the Internet may seem quite straightforward. In reality it's a very complex operation and the details fall outside the scope of this book.

The World Wide Web

As the Internet developed over the years so did the number of methods by which users could access information.

For the first 30 years of its existence the Net relied entirely on text-only ways of disseminating information, which was great if all that was required was to send e-mail or simple messages.

Access methods such as Telnet, which is used to log directly into a remote computer so that files and other information may be accessed, ruled the roost and because of slow modem speeds coupled with the small number of people accessing its services, there seemed no need to find more 'glamourous' access methods.

This view changed in the late 1980's when British scientist Tim Berners-Lee decided that a new approach was required to help him share data and information with his colleagues at the Particle Physics laboratory in Cern, Switzerland.

The new approach had hypertext at its core – a system which allows users to embed references to related information within a page, effectively allowing a page to contain its own index.

Berners-Lee had a number of working titles in mind for his new project including Information Mesh and Mine of Information but he eventually settled for the World Wide Web and in doing so launched a revolution which was to change the face of the Internet.

His idea included the creation of special instructions which would allow 'pages' of information to be delivered in digestible chunks which could be formatted to include a number of type styles ranging from bold to italics, paragraph breaks and even graphic images and sounds.

In the relatively few years since the original idea was first mooted the World Wide Web has come a long, long way.

Accessing the Web

The World Wide Web, and the Internet as a whole, relies on special computers called servers to make it work.

In reality these servers are ordinary computers of a very high specification with far more internal RAM memory than the average desktop PC and hard disk drives to match.

Their only purpose is to store vast quantities of information in the form of web page data, graphics and special programs which make the Web as we see it through a browser (see the next topic) work.

In order to access this information, Web users must request it using a special form of communication called the Hypertext Transfer Protocol, or HTTP for short.

Calls are made by typing a special web address into the web browser. This address is made in a standard format along the lines of:

http://www.computerstep.com/index.htm

This instruction contains several pieces of information vital to ensuring the correct data is retrieved and displayed.

The first part is the http:// which specifies that the information to be retrieved is Web data.

Next comes www.computerstep.com which is the name of the physical server on which the data sits.

Finally comes index.htm which is the name of the file to be retrieved from the server.

It works in a similar way to sending a letter. The http:// is the equivalent of the envelope, the www.computerstep.com is the 'street name' and the index.htm is the number of the house in the specified street. In order to access a given page of information on the web it is **essential** that the above format is used.

If it is not, the browser will be unable to find the correct information and may return some unwanted data – similar to the letter being delivered to the wrong address – or simply give up which may be likened to the letter being returned to the sender unopened.

HTTP is not the only Internet protocol available. Others include FTP or File Transfer Protocol which allows programs and files to be downloaded to the user's computer and TELNET which lets users directly access services and files on remote computers.

For smaller scale operations it is possible to use a home PC as a web server but to get the best out of this the computer in question needs to be connected to the Internet 24 hours a day – a costly operation!

However, for the purposes of developing websites and to learn more about how web servers work running your own – even if it isn't connected to the outside world – can be a valuable exercise.

The pick of the crop for the PC includes Microsoft's Personal Web Server which can be downloaded free of charge from http://www.microsoft.com and O'Reilly's Website which is available in free and pay-for versions from http://software.ora.com/

Web Browsers

Since its inception, the Web has been a very popular way of gathering information due to the ease with which data can be accessed and pages navigated.

But the success of this new medium doesn't rest solely on the shoulders of Tim Berners-Lee. Providing the information in an easy-to-program and easy-to-use form is one thing but it needs a specialist piece of computer software, called a browser, to interpret the information and display it in a suitable form.

Netscape's Navigator browser can be downloaded from http://www.netscape.com/, whilst its Microsoft competitor, Internet Explorer, can be found at http://www.microsoft.com/ie/

The creation of the first real web browser was the work of University of Illinois student Marc Andreeson who released a revolutionary product called Mosaic onto a waiting world.

The program immediately caught the imagination of the Internet community and led Andreeson to form NetScape Communications and create the highly popular Navigator series of web browsers which currently make up the vast majority of browsers accessing the web.

Sensing massive possibilities on the web, a large number of companies began to produce their own browser software across a wide variety of platforms, indeed it is possible to get a web browser for just about any computer with a hard disk these days.

Currently there are two major companies battling for supremacy of the browser market whilst at the same time constantly extending and amending specifications for the way the World Wide Web works.

One of these is, of course Netscape, the other is the mighty Microsoft empire with its Internet Explorer software.

HTML in Summary

HTML (HyperText Markup Language) is a specially designed markup language dedicated to helping web page designers display text and images with style and flair.

When compared to traditional programming languages, such as C and BASIC for example, it has relatively few commands making it easy for the novice to pick up whilst still providing enough versatility for the more experienced designer to pull off some very neat effects with very little effort.

This simplicity makes HTML a joy to learn and unlike its more technical peers it can be a very forgiving language, there are no unintelligible error messages and the code does not need to be compiled before it can be executed. HTML can be created in any text editor and placed directly into a browser resulting in instant display of content. There are currently a large number of packages which allow designers to build their pages in a WYSIWYG (What You See Is What You Get) form, giving an instant visual impression of what will appear (more on this in a moment).

Such rapid expansion does not come without a price however, and not all of the most recently introduced commands are compatible with all browsers – the new features of Internet Explorer 4 will not be found in the much older Netscape 2.0 or Microsoft's own earlier Internet Explorer 3 for example.

To find out much more about the latest developments in the HTML language visit the W3C at http://www.w3c.org

In an effort to control and standardise the extension of HTML the W3C, or World Wide Web Consortium was formed. Today, any extensions to the HTML language are referred to the W3C for inclusion into the official standard – a standard all developers are encouraged to adhere to in order to make their pages as accessible as possible.

Tools which may Help

There are many programs available today to help coders of all levels of skill to create pages for the web.

At the simplest level text editors such as the Windows Notepad/WordPad or BBEdit on the Apple Macintosh make perfectly acceptable HTML editing tools.

Increasingly, packages providing WYSIWYG (What You See Is What You Get) interfaces are being used by beginners. Such programs give the user an instant view of any changes they may make to their creations without the need to look at page after page of text-based instructions.

Such packages allow images to be dropped directly into an HTML page, allowing adjustments to be made onscreen until the designer is happy with the results.

Microsoft (http://www.microsoft.com) market the highly successful FrontPage series of editing packages. Whilst it is a commercial package, Frontpage provides a number of

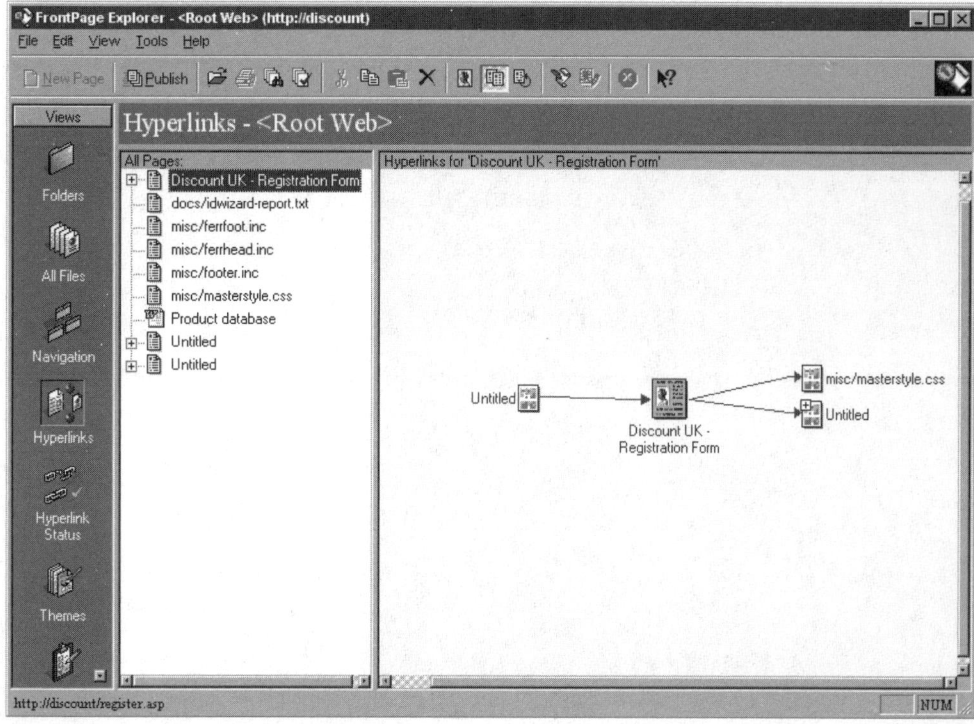

very useful tools for the designer including a full HTML creator and editor and even a web server, which allows a designers own computer to behave in the same way as a web server connected directly to the Net. In fact the server is so powerful that if a designer has a fast, permanent connection to the Internet the web server will send pages to anyone from any other Internet site in the world who requires them.

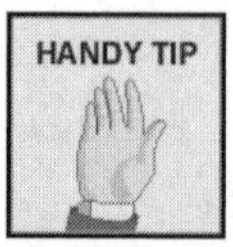

It's not essential to use high powered authoring tools to create HTML code. Any text editor or word processor will do the job. Just remember to always save your code in text format.

Those who prefer the more traditional approach to coding by using an extended text editor, Allaire (http://www.allaire.com) produce the very comprehensive HomeSite package.

At the end of the day choosing a package to suit is a very personal matter – what works for one person may be totally unsuitable for someone else.

For a first stop, try one of the many Shareware archives on the net, for example:

http://www.shareware.com

http://www.windows95.com

http://www.tucows.com

and for Macintosh users:

http://shell3.ba.best.com/~myee/umac/index.html

Chapter Two

Basic HTML

This chapter provides a look at the basic commands, or tags, that make up the core of the HTML language and allow designers to place text and images into a web page with the minimum of effort.

Covers

HTML Structure

As with any computer program, HTML documents must conform to a basic structure.

Thankfully the structure is an easy one to pick up and consists of only a small number of required elements.

The most obvious thing about HTML instructions, or tags as they are known, is the use of the angle brackets '<' and '>'. The brackets serve as delimiters, allowing anything between them to be interpreted as instructions relating to the way the page should be displayed rather than as parts of the page contents.

Other than the angle brackets, HTML requires little in the formal structure. A standard page consists of two main sections – a HEAD and a BODY.

The head is an 'invisible' portion of code which contains administrative information and any special scripts or codes your page may require. For many pages such information is not required and the head will contain only one HTML instruction, or tag as they are commonly known, the <TITLE>. The title is a simple line of text which describes or introduces the page and appears in the coloured bar at the top of your browser.

The majority of HTML tags come in pairs called containers. Containers are expressed as open tags i.e. <BODY> and close tags i.e. </BODY>.

The head is followed by the body of the document which is contained within the <BODY> and </BODY> tags. The body makes up the bulk of an HTML page and contains all of the text, images and other elements which are to appear.

The BODY tag is required by nearly all HTML files, the major exception being frame pages (more about this later).

The BODY tag can also contain a number of optional extras, or attributes, which allow for the setting up of colours, background images and other 'global' settings for the page. These include:

HTML was designed by the Americans so "colour" is spelt without the "u".

BGCOLOR

Fills the background of the page with a user defined colour. The colour setting can be expressed in one or two ways, either by name i.e. "blue" or "red" or as a six digit hexadecimal number (see the next topic).

BACKGROUND

Expands on the colour provision of BGCOLOR through the use of pictures, usually in GIF or JPG format, which fills the background of the browser over which the page contents will be displayed. If the visible area is larger than the image being loaded the browser will 'tile' the graphic, repeating it to fit all of the available space.

TEXT

Using the same colour conventions as BGCOLOR the TEXT tag allows the colour for standard body text to be changed.

LINK

Defines the colour of hyperlinks which have yet to be selected.

ALINK

Defines the colour of hyperlinks as they are being clicked.

VLINK

Defines the colour of hyperlinks which have already been visited.

BGPROPERTIES

Only available in some more modern browsers which 'watermarks' the page, fixing any image specified with the BACKGROUND tag so it does not move if a user scrolls up and down an HTML page.

Putting all of this together gives us the basic skeleton for all HTML documents:

```
<HTML>
<HEAD>
<TITLE>Welcome to my page</TITLE>
</HEAD>

<BODY BGCOLOR="BLUE" TEXT="WHITE"
 LINK="GREEN" ALINK="LIGHTGREEN"
 VLINK="DARKGREEN">

The bulk of your page goes in here
</BODY>
</HTML>
```

Tags can be written in upper case, lower case, or even mixed case. If you keep them consistently in capitals, they'll be easier to spot.

It is always important to remember that the bulk of HTML tags are expressed in pairs known as containers. Failing to close a container means the effect specified in the open part of that container will be carried out until a suitable close tag is found.

In the example above, if we forgot to include the </HEAD> tag the browser would assume all of the text was part of the head. As, generally speaking, information stored within the head is not displayed on the screen, nothing would appear.

One of the first things to check when any HTML code appears incorrectly is that all containers have their start and end positions correctly placed.

A Word About Colour Codes

The BGCOLOR, TEXT, LINK, ALINK AND VLINK tags may all use hexadecimal notation to describe the colours that represent them.

Based around base 16 numbers, Hexadecimal, or hex as it is commonly known, expands on our usual number system called decimal, or base 10. As we all know, base 10 numbers are represented by the digits 0 to 9. Hex provides the facility to expand this to represent the numbers from 0 to 15 by using the letters A through to F for numbers higher than 9. Thus 10 is represented by A, 11 by B, 12 by C and so on.

Numbers beyond 15 get a little trickier. In decimal, the number 16 would be expressed using one amount of ten and one amount of six. In hex, because it allows numbers to 15 through the use of A through F, 16 is expressed as 10 – one amount of 16 and no other digits.

As you may guess telling the difference between 16 and 10 is a confusing one – is that a normal 10 or a 16 in hexadecimal?, so to make things easier, those wonderful people who set the standard for hexadecimal notation have given us a # (hash) symbol to denote situations when hex is being used – hence the number 132 in decimal is written as #84 (eight lots of 16 and 4) in hexadecimal.

So far so good, but what has this to do with colours? This form of hex notation is extremely useful when describing colour as today's browsers express colour values using the RGB format. Confused? Well it's not as complicated as it may first appear.

Every colour that can be displayed by the browser is made up of three elements: Red, Green and Blue and each of these three colour elements has a value between 0 and 255 (#00 and #FF in hexadecimal).

By assigning values for each element we can achieve different colours. For example a value of #FF0000 would result in pure red (FF for maximum red followed by 00 levels of green and 00 levels of blue). Similarly #00FF00 would give pure green, #0000FF pure blue, #000000 black and #FFFFFF pure white. By using this system an amazing number of colours and shades can be created to fit almost any occasion or design situation.

In creating wild and lurid colour schemes for your pages it is important to remember that many web surfers have their browsers set up to handle the standard 256 colour palette which contains 216 colours which have been termed 'browser safe'. Using colours outside of this range may mean that viewers with older browsers may see slightly different results to those you intended.

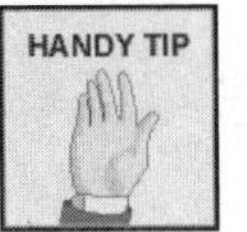

For a full list of the 216 "browser safe" colours visit http://www.limitless.co.uk/colour/colour.html

Some common colour values:

Red	FF0000
Green	00FF00
Blue	0000FF
Yellow	FFFF00
Orange	FFA500
Gold	FFD700
Beige	F5F5DC
Gray	808080
Navy	000080
Black	000000
White	FFFFFF

Note: The numerically aware among you may have realised that with 256 levels each of red, green and blue available there are potentially millions of colours which can be displayed. The only way to ensure you achieve the desired colour is to play with the colour values until you hit upon something you're looking for. Have fun!

Paragraphs

In order to help designers make text on a page look more presentable use the <P>, or paragraph tag.

The <P> tag tells the browser to finish rendering the current area of text, insert a carriage return and follow it with a blank line before continuing.

There is no way in standard HTML to force the text to align with both margins - a process sometimes referred to as justification.

The end result is similar to what you see on this page, the text is nicely spaced and there are plenty of empty lines to help differentiate between individual paragraphs.

There are two ways to use the paragraph tag, both work equally well and it's a matter of taste as to which you adopt.

In the first instance just pop a <P> at the end of the area you are working with. For example: The end of this paragraph is approaching now<p>.

The second way involves the use of the tag with its accompanying </P>, creating a container pair as in: <P>Here's another way to do it</P>. Although it may seem a little long-winded this approach is more in line with the standards for HTML code creation as set down by the W3C.

Either way of expressing the paragraph is suitable but the latter example is slightly more flexible in that it will give the designer a little more control over his or her layout allowing the use of alignment tags through the ALIGN command.

ALIGN isn't recognized by some of the older browsers but should be fine in the majority. It has three settings; LEFT which positions the text to the left hand edge of the page, RIGHT which positions it to the right and CENTER which centres the paragraph within the page.

Careful use of ALIGN in conjunction with the paragraph can by itself create some interesting effects when used with text only pages or sites.

The following code fragment can be used to demonstrate effective use of the align attribute:

```
<html>
<head>
<title>My Test Page</title>
</head>

<body>
<p align=left>This paragraph has been aligned to the left hand
side of the browser using the align attribute of the paragraph
tag</p>
<p align=right>This paragraph has been aligned to the left hand
side of the browser using the align attribute of the paragraph
tag</p>
<p align=center>This paragraph has been aligned to the centre
of the browser using the align attribute of the paragraph tag</
p>
</body>
</html>
```

Which produces:

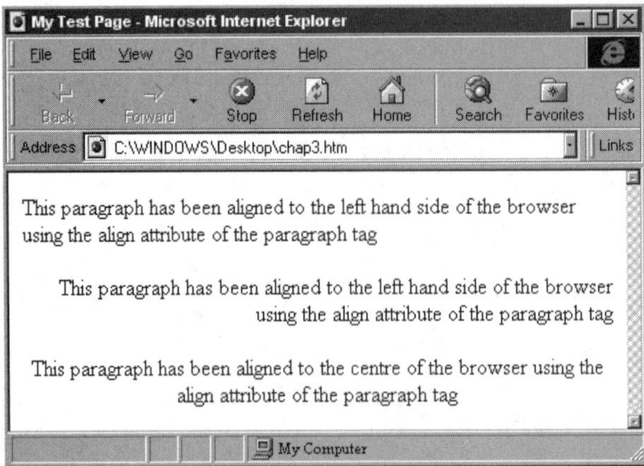

Line Breaks

There are times when a paragraph break may seem inconvenient and all that's required is a break which will finish the current line of text and start a new one directly underneath without leaving the kind of space created using a <P> tag.

HTML provides the <BR>, or line break tag, for this purpose.

The <BR> tag is one of a small number of HTML tags which are used in isolation. The bulk of HTML's components are known as containers, using a start tag, for example <P> with an end tag </P> to provide a container. The <BR>, however, is not a container but merely a break and therefore does not require (and should not be used with) a </BR> tag.

As with the paragraph tag, the <BR> carries a couple of useful options which can come in handy when designing pages which contain images.

Sometimes it's handy to be able to place an image on a page and to ensure that accompanying text doesn't begin at the side of it, but underneath. The attributes which allow such actions are:

CLEAR

Allows designers to restart the text given certain conditions.

CLEAR=RIGHT

Holds the text until the right margin is cleared.

CLEAR=LEFT

Holds it until the left is free.

CLEAR=ALL

Ensures there are no images restricting the text on either side before placing more on the page.

Text alignment can be a tricky thing to visualise so here's a brief example of how it works:

```
This is an example of how the line break can be used to force
text to fit around images on an HTML page.<p>
<img src="logo.gif" align=left>
This text sits to the right of the image. By placing a &lt;BR
CLEAR=LEFT&gt; at the end of this portion of text, the
following text will not start until the left margin is clear.<br
clear=left>
Excellent! The browser has now detected the left margin is clear
of images and other obstructions to the text flow.<p>
<img src="logo.gif" align=right>
This time around we'll wait for the right margin to be cleared by
using the &lt;BR CLEAR=RIGHT&gt;.
<br clear=right>
And now the right margin is clear of obstructions...
```

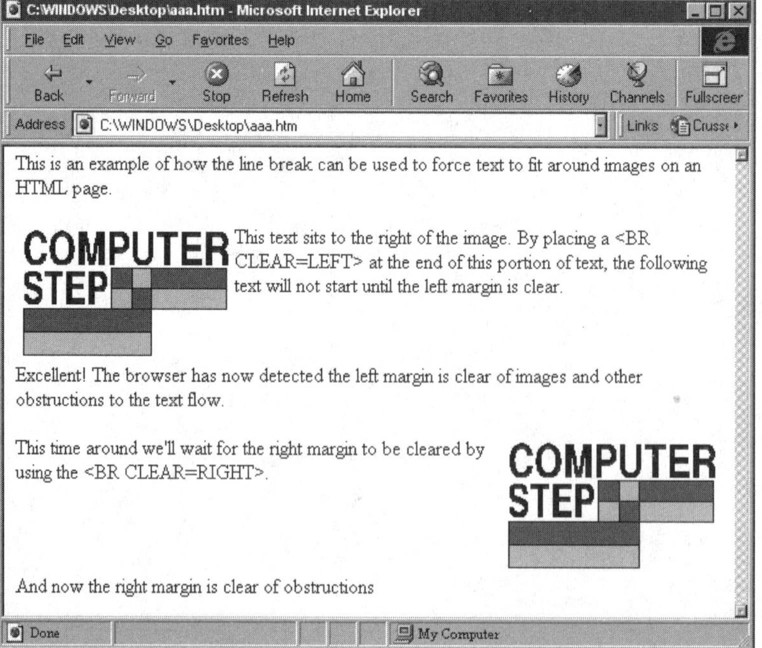

Headings and Font Sizes

Headings

HTML provides for a basic range of text sizes as defined by the heading or <H> containers.

Six predefined heading sizes are provided ranging from <H1> which is the biggest through to <H7>.

The headings are provided in such a way that H1 is used for major headings, H2 for subheadings, H3 for sub-subheadings and so on in a sliding scale to H7 which is very small.

More Font Control

From the introduction of Netscape Navigator version 2, a further tag was added which allows for relative control over font sizes within a document. From this point on headings were no longer restricted to the seven sizes dictated by the heading tag but could be set relative to the default font size.

For example, to create text in a size slightly larger than the current default, designers can add <FONT SIZE=+1> to their code. Larger still was <FONT SIZE=+2>. By using a minus sign instead of the plus the font sizes can be decreased – <FONT SIZE=-1> will display text in a size one smaller than the current.

As a further extension, selective use of colours can be applied by adding the COLOR= attribute.

<FONT COLOR="RED"> for example renders any text which follows in the appropriate colour. Note that the COLOR function also allows for the use of hexadecimal RGB values as discussed earlier.

The final attribute for the FONT tag is the FACE attribute which allows designers to break away from the browser default typeface and use another in its place.

Designers can feel free to use any font they choose but it is important to remember that the visitor to a page must have the same fonts on their machine in order for this command to have any effect. If the specified font is not available the text will be displayed in the default typeface.

Efforts can be made to combat this by specifying several faces separated by commas. If this approach is used, the browser will start with the first name in the list and work through each until it reaches one it can find on the client machine.

For example:

```
<font face="arial, chicago, jurassic">This text will be displayed
in a non-standard font</font>
```

will force the browser to check for the existence of a typeface called arial. If it's not present the browser will then search for chicago and finally jurassic. If none of the faces are available the default font will be used.

Pages should never be designed around a specific font as it is impossible to guarantee that font will be present on every machine which is used to visit the page and use of fancy fonts should be regarded as an optional extra rather than as a necessity.

This is H1

This is H2

This is H3

This is H4

This is H5

This is H6

This is the default font size

... and this is what happens when we use <FONT SIZE=+1>

<FONT SIZE=+2> is even bigger

Other Layout Controls

In addition to giving control over the text size, HTML gives a broad range of options for the way that any text is rendered on the page. These are given below, but note that each of the tags below has a corresponding end tag:

<B>	Bold
<I>	Italics
<SUP>	superscript
<SUB>	subscript
<U>	underline
<STRIKE>	strikethrough
<BIG>	makes the text one size bigger
<SMALL>	makes the text one size smaller
<TT>	Displays the text in monospaced type
<EM>	Emphasises the text (usually in italics)
<STRONG>	Strong text (usually bold)
<DFN>	Displays a definition
<CODE>	Displays text as program code
<SAMP>	Sample output from a program
<KBD>	Used for text a user may enter at the keyboard
<VAR>	Used for variables from a program
<CITE>	Used for references and citations
<ADDRESS>	Usually used to contain the address details of the page author, which may be home, phone number, email or other.

<BLOCKQUOTE>

Any text placed between <BLOCKQUOTE> and </BLOCKQUOTE> is paragraphed and indented to make it stand out from the rest of the text body. Placing a blockquoted section of text within a <BLOCKQUOTE> area will increase the size of the indent.

<DIV>

Creates a text DIVision. DIVs allow the use of the align tag for instances where special text effects may be required.

For example a DIV with the attribute ALIGN=RIGHT will display the text aligned to the right hand edge of the page.

BEWARE

Spell "CENTER" the American way as shown here rather than as "CENTRE".

<CENTER>

Text lines contained by the <CENTER> tag will be centred within the width of the browser.

<PRE>

A very useful tag for displaying preformatted text. When text held in an HTML document is displayed to the screen any extra spaces, line breaks and tab characters are omitted from the text. Sometimes, for example when displaying recipes and the like, it's important to be able to insert such special characters for formatting reasons.

When a web browser deals with text held between the <PRE> and </PRE> tags it will display that text 'as is' making no attempt to remove any extra characters it encounters.

Hyperlinks

The World Wide Web would be a dull place indeed if it were not for hyperlinks. Without hyperlinks it wouldn't be possible to navigate around a users website or to 'jump off' to other places around the Internet.

In order to allow the designer to include hyperlinks within a page, HTML provides the <A> or anchor container. The anchor is always used with a </A> close tag.

This command is usually to be found in the form:

```
<a href="http://www.computerstep.com">some text here</a>
```

utilizing the HREF attribute which contains the name of the page the browser will jump to when the hyperlink is clicked.

Care should always be taken to ensure that all of the links included within a page are working properly. There is nothing more frustrating to a Net surfer than finding an interesting link on a page, clicking it and then finding the page designer has supplied the wrong address.

The anchor tag can also be used to point visitors to particular points in the current page, or *bookmarks* as they are known.

Setting a bookmark requires the use of the second attribute of the anchor, the NAME, in the form

```
<A NAME="mybookmark">
```

– it does of course require an </A> to close if off.

In order to reference the bookmark a variant of the <A HREF= ... > is used at the relevant point in the page to point to the pre-defined bookmark.

In order to differentiate a bookmark from a reference to another page the hash symbol (#) is added at the start of the HREF reference which tells the browser the link is within the current HTML document.

The following code segment demonstrates the use of the standard off-page reference and a reference to a bookmark within the current page:

```
<HTML>
<HEAD>
<TITLE>Bookmark Reference example</TITLE>
</HEAD>
<BODY>
<A HREF="http://www.computerstep.com">Click here to go
to the Computer Step website</a><P>
<A HREF="#mytext">Click here to go to the bookmark called
mytext</a>
This text forms the bulk of the current page and it goes here and
will, without doubt, be very interesting.<P>
<a name="mytext">This is the point where the bookmark
called mytext sits. When the visitor clicks on the link above the
browser will display this text at the top of the display area</a>
</body>
</html>
```

Using bookmarks within a single page is a very useful technique if that page contains a lot of text, as it saves the visitor from having to scroll through all that goes before in order to get to desired sections.

It is possible to send a user to a bookmark on a separate page using a combination of the above techniques. For example:

```
<a href="http://www.mysite.com/mypage.html#mymark">
```

will send the user to the bookmark mymark on the page mypage.html at the site http://www.mysite.com.

Not all hyperlinks take the visitor to other pages or to bookmarks, sometimes it's useful to use the last trick up the hyperlink's sleeve which is to use it to allow email to be sent.

In this instance the <A HREF= is married up with the special MAILTO: command to produce a slightly odd looking command which, when clicked, will automatically invoke the visitors email package and allow them to send you a message.

For example:

```
<A HREF="MAILTO:me@here.com">Email me with
comments</A>
```

will start an email package and enter the email address me@here.com in the to: field. You'll often find this command at the foot of a page asking for comments on a particular site.

Horizontal Rules

Now and again it's nice to insert a rule into a page of text to break it up a little. The <HR> tag (note there is no /HR>) performs this job and comes complete with these attributes:

WIDTH

The width of the rule can be expressed two ways. Firstly as a number – <HR WIDTH=500> would give a line 500 pixels long and secondly as a percentage of the available screen width – <HR WIDTH=75%> would render a line to that value.

SIZE

Allows the designer to specify how high, in pixels, the line will be.

NOSHADE

By default horizontal rules come with a 3D look. By using NOSHADE the line is displayed without the drop shadow that would normally accompany the basic line.

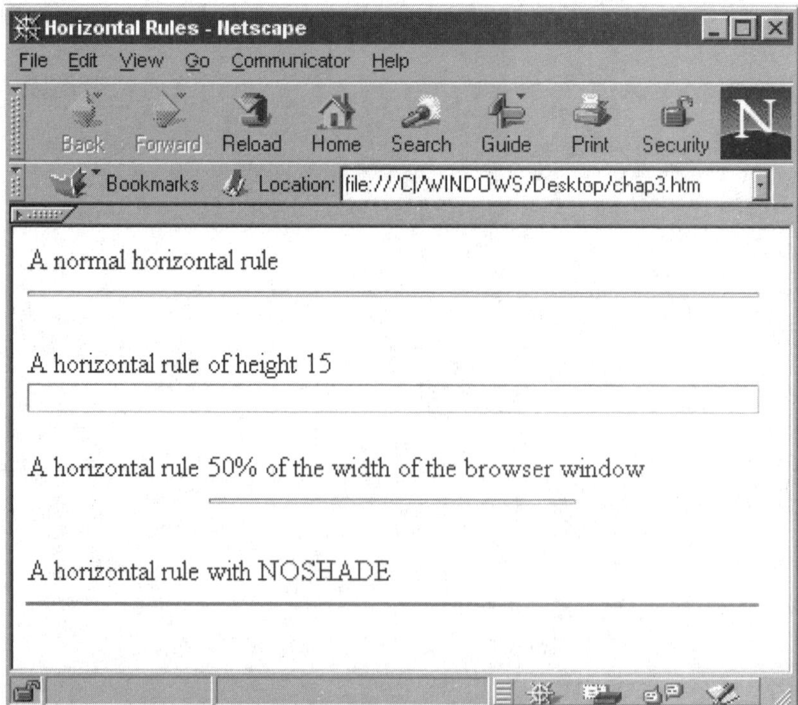

Lists

HTML provides specialist tags for presenting text in the form of lists. All lists on a HTML page are constructed the same way, only the style of presentation differs.

Unordered Lists

The simplest kind of list is the unordered list which presents each line of the list with its own bullet point. Unordered lists are defined between the <UL> and </UL> tags and each entry must begin with a <LI> (list item) tag.

Ordered Lists

Ordered lists are displayed in the same fashion as their unordered counterparts with one exception – ordered lists replace bullet points with numbers. Use the <OL> and </OL> containers to indicate an ordered list. The browser will work out the numbering scheme automatically.

Lists are usually rendered with an indent from the left margin of the page. Placing a list within a list will result in an extension of the indent.

Lists - an example

```
<UL>
    <LI>Option 1
    <LI>Option 2
    <LI>Option 3
        <OL>
            <li>No bullets!
            <li>Just numbers!
        </OL>
</UL>
```

When displayed in a browser the code segment on the opposite page will produce the following results. Note the bullets on options one through three which were defined as unordered list items as opposed to the final two embedded list items, which were set up as an ordered list.

- Option 1
- Option 2
- Option 3
    1. No bullets!
    2. Just numbers!

Finally...

The last two kinds of lists have been all but phased out of the newer versions of HTML but are worthy of note for the sake of completeness.

The <DIR> and <MENU> list types were originally intended to display text as DIRectory or MENU items. As such both list types were designed to handle very short descriptions or phrases similar to that which might appear in DOS or UNIX style directory listings or on-screen menus.

In reality the work of these list types can be easily handled using the ordered and unordered list tags so they have been gradually phased out as the HTML specification has advanced. It is expected that by the time the W3C finally ratify the standard for HTML version 4 the <DIR> and <MENU> tags will have been removed completely.

Comments

The final tag to be discussed in this section doesn't do anything. At all.

However, even though it doesn't do anything it can be a useful tool.

The comment tag allows the designer to add messages and remarks into a section of HTML code which explains what that code does.

Comments are expressed using the <!-- and --> container pair. Anything that appears within the containers is not displayed onscreen.

There are two practical applications for the comment which stand out above all others.

The first is in adding explanatory comments to complex code or statements. Quite often web pages will be updated over time and going back to something written weeks or months beforehand can result in much head scratching as you try to grasp just exactly what it is you originally wrote. A quick comment included at the time of writing can often make things clearer.

Secondly, the comment can be used to mask off sections of code that are not needed or need to be disabled for some reason. Say, for example you have a menu of five options, some of which are not applicable for the next few weeks. Rather than removing the code to display the menu option it's sometimes easier to comment it out so it can be reintroduced later on.

For example:

```
<!-- What follows will not appear onscreen
<font size=+1 color="red">I'm some onscreen text</font>
End of the comment area here -->
```

and

```
<!-- Code written Feb 24 to display a menu -->
```

Displaying Extended Characters

The letters, numbers and other symbols that can be displayed within an HTML page are known as the character set.

This collection of symbols, which are available directly from a computer keyboard are (obviously) essential in getting a message across.

But there are times when it's just not enough.

As we've already seen HTML reserves some symbols for its own use. The 'less than' and 'greater than' symbols (< and >) are used to differentiate between page text and HTML tags for example.

And then there are the foreign characters and special symbols such as the copyright and the registered trademark symbol which are available for use within HTML pages but not obviously available from the keyboard.

In order to access such symbols we have to use a special shorthand code which starts with the ampersand (&) and ends with a semicolon (;).

There are far too many to list all of them here, but below are a few which you may find useful.

<	<	>	>
©	©	®	®
½	½	¼	¼
¾	¾	À	à
Â	â	Ä	ä
Æ	æ	È	è
Ê	ê	à	à

There is one final code which can be very useful – this is the non-breaking space or . As a rule, HTML ignores multiple spaces in text, acknowledging only the first if several appear in succession. Using the   inserts the spaces into the text.

Basic HTML – An Example

```
<html>
<head>                                                    1
<title>CS Home Page</title>
</head>
<body background="images/brntxtr2.jpg">                   2
<img src="images/homer.gif" width="80"
height="16"><a href="whatsnew.htm">
<img src="images/new.gif" border="0"                      3
width="80" height="16"></a><p>
<img src="images/logo.gif" width="168"
height="98"><p>
<font color="#000080" size="5" face="MS Sans
Serif"><strong>W                                          4
E L C O M E</strong></font><p>
<font size="3">to Computer Step... the leading British    5
publisher of computer books.</font>
<br><br>
<img src="images/div.gif" alt="Dividing Line Image"       6
width="496" height="7"><em><br>
<img src="images/MailC241.gif" width="32"                 7
height="32"> Computer Step . Southfield Road .
Southam . Warwickshire CV33 OFB .England</
em><br>
<font size="1" face="MS Sans Serif"><strong>Tel: </
strong></font><font size="3"><em>+44 (0)1926
817999</em></font>
<font size="1" face="MS Sans Serif"><strong>Fax</
strong>:</font> <em>+44 (0)1926 817005</
em><br>
<font size="1" face="MS Sans Serif"><strong>E-
Mail:</strong></font>
```

```
<a href="mailto:webmaster@computerstep.com">            8
webmaster@computerstep.com</a>

<a href="http://www.microsoft.com/ie"><font size="1"
face="MS Sans Serif"><strong><img src="images/        9
ie_animated.gif" border="0" width="88"
Height="31"></strong>  </font></a>
</body>                                                  10
</html>
```

The breakdown of the above is:

1 The HEAD portion of the page including the TITLE.

2 Declares the start of the page BODY, a background image is described as well as a background colour.

3 Displays an image called Homer followed by a second called new.gif which has been surrounded with a hyperlink tag (some code has been cut for the sake of clarity).

4 Displays a welcome message after setting properties for the text.

5 The main portion of the text (cut for clarity).

6 Displays a graphic which is used as a horizontal line on the page.

7 Another image with accompanying text.

8 Sets up a mailto: hyperlink which will automatically start a suitable mail program when the link is clicked.

9 The final image declaration of the page.

10 The BODY and HTML opening containers are closed here.

And when it's all put together the final result is this:

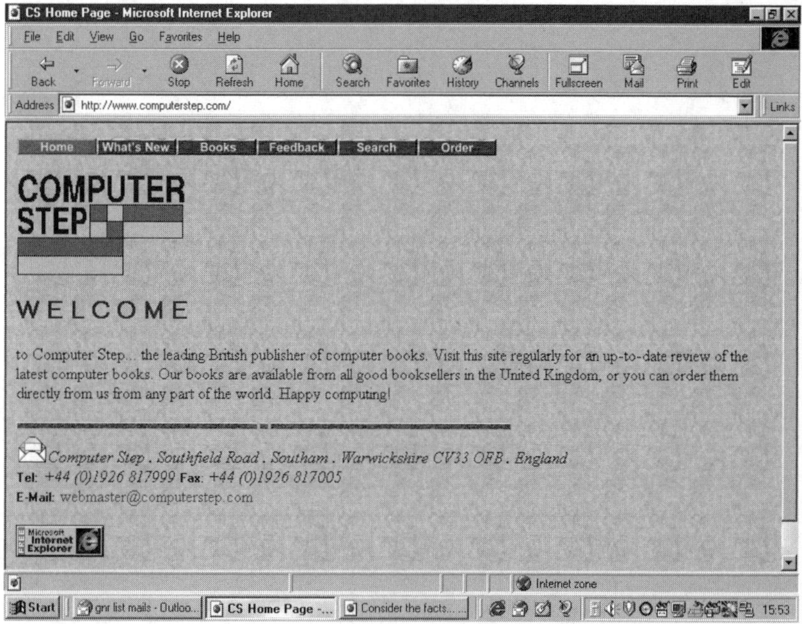

Online Resources

There's always room when writing HTML for a little help and advice from others. Listed below are a handful of sites which contain excellent online resources and a hatful of hints and tips to help you on your way when designing pages.

http://web.syr.edu/~mkarjoo/www/

http://sunflower.singnet.com.sg/~klien/html.htm - links page

http://www.xs4all.nl/~waxxie/1010tips/noframes/ - Studio 10/10

http://www.hwg.org/ - HTML Writers Guild

http://www.stars.com/Authoring/HTML/Tutorial/

Chapter Three

Using Images

There comes a time in every web designer's experience when text alone is simply not enough and graphics are required to liven up a design.

From the simplest of buttons to the elaborate logo, graphics can transform a plain page of text into something rich and vibrant which will make your site stand head and shoulders above those of others. As with everything else, HTML affords a good degree of control over images and how they are displayed, allowing designers to let their imaginations run riot.

Covers

The <IMG> tag

In common with almost all elements of an HTML page, graphics have their own tag – <IMG>.

Placing a graphic onto a page is no more difficult than using the <IMG> tag in its most basic form – <IMG SRC="mygraphic.gif">. The first part of the tag tells the browser to expect an image, the second part gives it the name of the file to use – in this case mygraphic.gif (more on GIFs in a moment).

What this segment of code will do is to place an image with the default left justification. Any text around the graphic in the HTML file will be placed onscreen above and below the selected image, which is functional if a little boring. In order to make it more interesting we are provided with the ALIGN attribute which can take three values – LEFT, RIGHT or CENTER. Adding any to an IMG tag not only places the image flush to the left or right page margins (or centres it between the two) but tells the browser to flow the text around the image, leaving the kind of effect you might expect from a printed magazine.

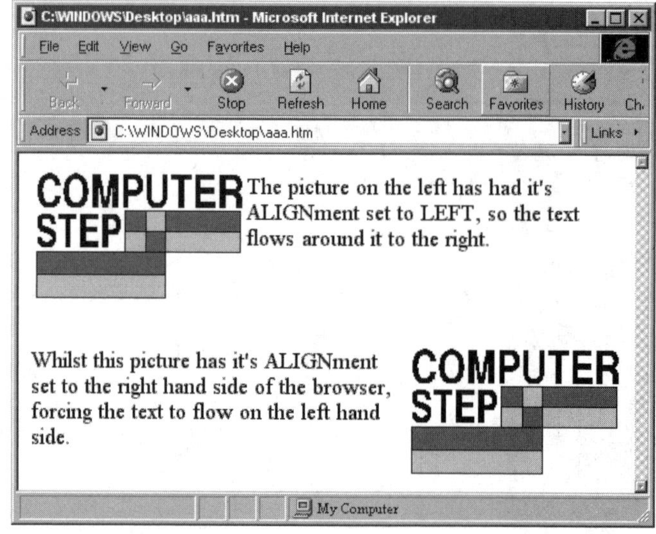

In addition images can be scaled at the time they are placed on the page using the optional HEIGHT= and WIDTH= attributes which allow the designer to explicitly set a size for the image as it will appear. Specifying the height and width for an image allows the browser to set aside a given amount of space for it on the page as that page is being built.

The advantage of using these attributes is that the browser knows in advance how much space to set aside for the image, allowing the page as a whole to be built more quickly than if the attributes had been omitted.

A third attribute, ALT, provides for situations where visitors may have images switched off or for those who may be viewing a site with a text only browser. The ALT tag allows designers to attach a text description to an image which is displayed if, and only if, the visitor has decided not to have images displayed. Using the ALT tag helps designers to allow for all possible situations and it is recommended that it is included in any page design.

Putting all of the above together gives us a tag which reads:

```
<IMG SRC="mycat.gif" WIDTH=100 HEIGHT=75
ALIGN=RIGHT ALT="A picture of my cat Manic">
```

which will place the graphic file called mycat.gif on the right of the browser with dimensions of 100 by 75 and display the text "A picture of my cat Manic" if image viewing has been turned off.

Finally, there are two attributes which allow the designer to put space between the edge of the image and the surrounding text.

HSPACE and VSPACE both take numeric values which specify the amount of horizontal and vertical space surrounding any image they are applied to. This value is specified in pixels.

File Types – GIF, JPG and PNG

There are many different types of graphic format available in the electronic world today, each with its own strengths and weaknesses.

For the purposes of the Internet, and more specifically the Web, the choice boils down to either GIF (Graphic Interchange Format) or JPG (Joint Picture Experts Group). The GIF and JPG formats provide the best balance between small file sizes – always useful when trying to create a page that can be downloaded quickly even by the slowest of modems – and picture quality.

The GIF format was created by the people at the online service CompuServe as a means of transmitting graphics over modem lines. They are restricted in terms of the number of colours they may contain, a maximum of 256, but compress very well, allowing high quality for little file size. As a result of the colour weakness of this format it is best suited to non-photographic images such as pictures created from scratch in graphics packages.

JPGs on the other hand are very good for storing photo quality images. They use different compression techniques to that of the GIF and is aimed towards the photographic end of the graphics spectrum. Unfortunately, this specialisation means that the very thing GIF does best – displaying lower quality images with few colours – is poorly handled by JPG. So it's best to use them for scans or images taken from digital cameras.

HANDY TIP

Learn more about the PNG format by visiting http://www.cdrom.com/pub/png/

As with all things Internet-related there is a newcomer on the block in the form of the PNG (Portable Network Graphic) format.

PNG combines all of the best attributes of GIF and JPG in one compact form. However, at the time of writing, the number of browsers which provide support for this new format is very small and it is unlikely to make a major impact in the foreseeable future.

Extending the GIF format

Whilst it may at first seem that GIF is the poor cousin of JPG there's actually a lot more to it. The GIF format has several cunning tricks up its sleeve which make it more versatile than its opponent and therefore infinitely more suited to some instances.

Transparency

Using an extension of the original GIF format, GIF89A allows users to declare one colour in an image palette to be transparent.

The effect of this, when the image is placed on a webpage, is that all of the other colours in the image appear as normal but the selected colour is totally see-through. The advantages of this are obvious as it allows whatever is behind the image – usually the background colour or background image to show through allowing a number of interesting graphical effects to be created.

Interlaced GIFs

Ordinarily graphic files are displayed from the top down appearing line by line as the data is loaded into the computers memory.

This can make it very hard to see what the image is going to be, especially over slow Internet connections and in instances where large images are used.

In order to combat this, interlaced GIFs may be used. An interlaced GIF is displayed in a slightly different fashion with every third of fourth line appearing. The image seems to go through several 'passes' as the graphic builds up – to begin with the 1st, 4th and 7th lines may appear followed by lines 2, 5 and 8 and finally 3, 6 and 9. The beauty of such a technique is that the visitor gets an impression of what the image is from the outset without a lengthy wait for the whole image to load.

Animating GIFs

The final trick up the GIF's sleeve is its ability to store multiple frames in one file, allowing designers to create an animated effect similar to the flick picture books many of us had as children. By far the easiest way to achieve this is by using a package especially designed for creating such graphics – like Microsoft's GIF animator.

The first stage of the operation is really the tricky bit and that involves creating each frame of your sequence. Once this is done it's time to open the GIF animation package and get down to the interesting stuff.

The frames which make up the animation are shown here

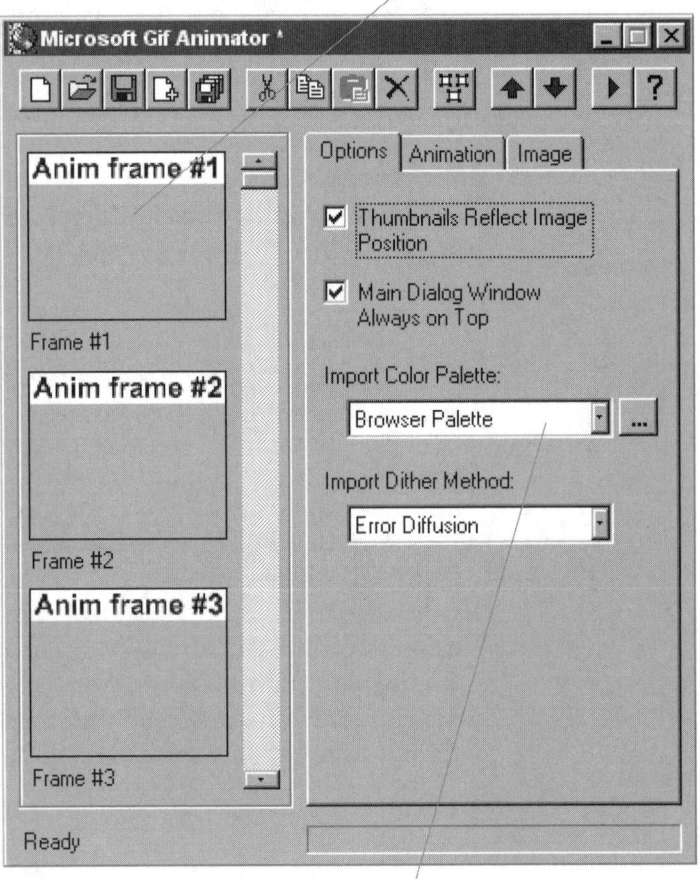

Allows you to specify colour palettes for your creations

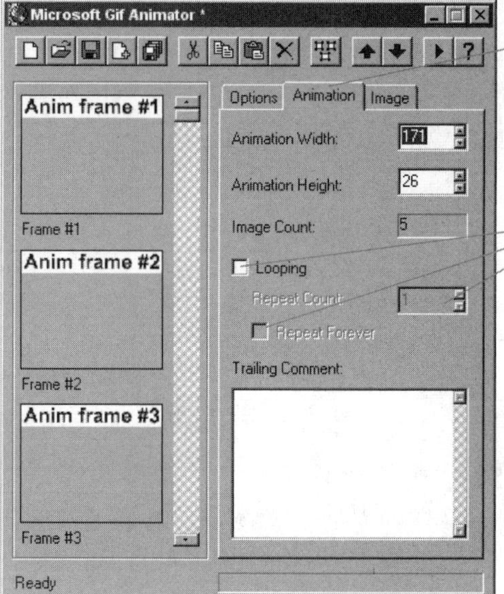

This box deals with the details of the animation itself

These options allow the designer to set how many times the animation will repeat. Clicking 'Forever' will force the animation to continue indefinitely

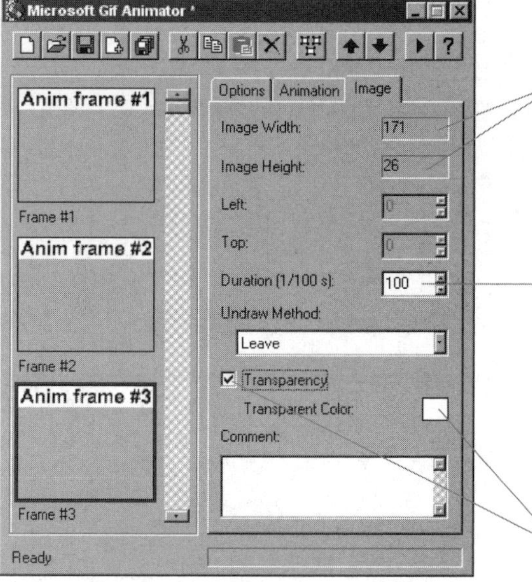

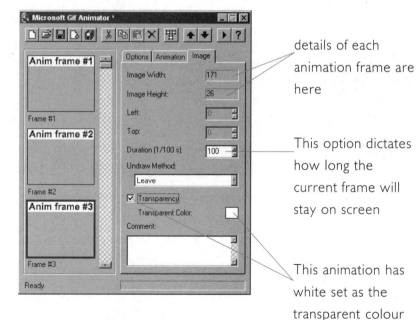

details of each animation frame are here

This option dictates how long the current frame will stay on screen

This animation has white set as the transparent colour

Image Maps

We saw in the last chapter that text elements of an HTML page can be 'wrapped' within the <A HREF> construct to allow designers to add hyperlinks into their creations, and using image maps we can do the same for graphics.

Sometimes a plain list of text links won't fit into a design and it's desirable to use a whizz-bang graphic to do the job instead. The problem with this is that the single graphic may represent more than one link and the <A HREF> tag will only allow us one connection. Using an image map we can tell the browser that particular sections of the graphic, when clicked, will trigger a jump to a particular page.

Background

There are two types of image map which can be used in a web page, one which relies on information stored on the server, the other which is run through the browser, or client.

Server side image mapping is the older technique of the two and is compatible with all browsers. It relies on information being passed back to the server when a visitor clicks on a map. The information is translated and the relevant link is passed back and acted upon by the browser. The problem with this approach centres around the amount of data which needs to pass between the server and the browser just to discover which link has been selected.

Much more effective and efficient, is to use client-side image maps. With a client-side map, all of the data required to operate the selection procedure is included with the HTML page, cutting out the need for streams of communication with the server.

Creating a Client-side map

A client side image map (csim) is made up of two elements: the graphical map and the code which tells the browser how to operate it.

The map needs to be created using a graphics package. Once this has been completed the serious business of providing the code to run it can begin.

The code itself requires two elements, the <IMG> tag which will display the map and the <MAP> declaration which provides instructions on what it will do.

The <IMG> tag is very similar to a normal declaration, taking all of the attributes discussed earlier in this chapter for the positioning and sizing of the graphic. However, there are two extra attributes – ISMAP, which tells the browser this is an image map and USEMAP which contains an anchor link to the map definition data (we'll get to that in a moment). For example:

```
<IMG SRC="mymap.gif" WIDTH=100 HEIGHT=100 ISMAP
USEMAP="#mapdata">
```

The map data sits inside the <MAP> container and looks something like this:

```
<MAP NAME="mapdata">
<AREA ...>
<AREA ...>
<AREA ...>
</MAP>
```

The important thing here is that the map definition contains a number of AREA definitions, each of which sets up areas of the graphic map which will trigger active links when the mouse pointer moves over them.

The attributes for the AREA tag are:

SHAPE
One of “RECT”, “CIRCLE”, “POLY” or “DEFAULT”. The first three options define the hotspot as a standard shape, “DEFAULT” allows the designer to specify an action for instances where none of the user-defined shapes have been selected.

COORDS
Specifies sets of X and Y coordinates within the map image that will act as hotspots. When the mouse moves over a hotspot the browser detects that a link has been activated. If a mouse button is pressed the browser will act in the same way as if a hyperlink has been selected.

HREF
Contains the URL the browser will jump to when the hotspot is clicked by the page visitor.

Putting all of these together gives:

```
<AREA SHAPE="RECT" COORDS="100,100,200,200"
HREF="http://www.apage.co.uk">
```

Creating an image map may sound like a complicated process but thanks to some inventive programmers there are several good packages which can do all the hard work. For PC users there is the very excellent Map This package.

Creating an Image Map using Map This
Putting together an image map by hand is a time consuming and very tricky process. It requires a good eye on the part of the designer for the difficult procedure of deciding just where the coordinates of the various hotspots will be and any mistakes can take a long time to rectify. It's a good job then that there are easy-to-use tools which can take all of the pain out of image map creation.

MapThis can be downloaded as freeware from http:// www.mapthis.com

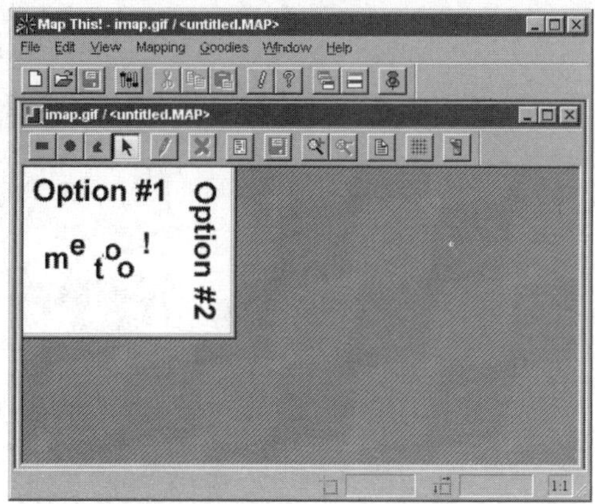

Here, we've loaded a simple example map into MapThis which contains three areas which will become the hotspots.

Using the tools just above the map the hotspots have been marked out. If any of them is wrongly placed or needs to be resized that can be done now.

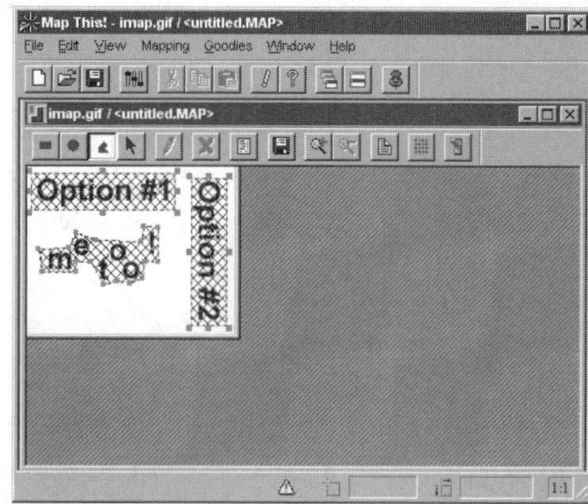

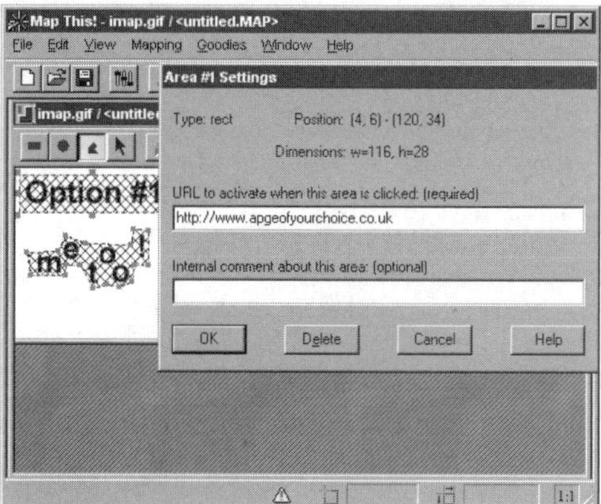

Once the hotspots have been set up, it's time to give details of where each will point.

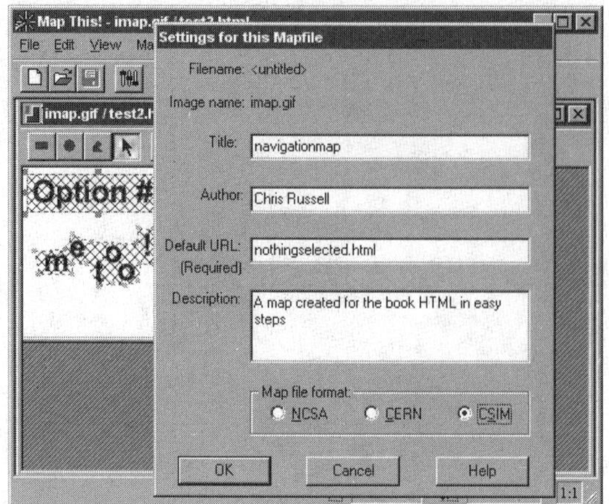

The final stage allows for the naming of the map. The box at the foot of the page allows for the creation of maps as server-side or client-side objects.

And after this simple procedure here's the code that was created:

```
<BODY>
<MAP NAME="navigationmap">
<!-- Descriptive code & comments cut for clarity -->
<AREA SHAPE=RECT COORDS="4,6,120,134" HREF="http://pageofyourchoice.co.uk">
<AREA SHAPE=RECT COORDS="135,10,163,125"
HREF="http://www.anotherpage.co.uk">
<AREA SHAPE=POLY
COORDS="9,65,34,64,40,52,56,58,92,59,94,47,106,48,
106,75,95,75,93,88,83,92,73,90,62,93,52,75,40,75,40,83,12,83,9,65"
HREF="http://anotherpageonmysite.html">
<AREA SHAPE=default HREF="nothingselected.html">
</MAP>
</BODY>
```

Sourcing Images for your Designs

There are a myriad of ways in which suitable graphical material can be obtained for use in web pages. The most straightforward is to create them yourself using one of the many graphic packages which are available today.

Graphics creation is a whole discipline in itself and would take a book far bigger than this one to get to the bottom of.

Sources of inspiration for graphics designs can come from any number of places and a couple of hours scouring the Net and examining the work of others can often give rise to a wide variety of ideas for the designer looking for something a little different.

Another way is to use a scanner, a device which takes existing images on paper, or from books or magazines and turns them into digital images. Digital cameras can be used to take electronic snapshots which can then be incorporated into a design. You can even take graphics from the websites of others if they take your fancy but there is a huge word of warning here concerning copyright. If you do see something you like that belongs to someone else or comes from an existing website always ask before using it.

It is **VERY IMPORTANT** to understand that just taking someone's work without asking first may constitute a breach of copyright law and in extreme cases could even land you in court.

If you are in any doubt about the source of graphics (or text or sounds for that matter) do not use them and create your own instead. Besides it's much more gratifying knowing that your finished production really is all your own work.

Programs which may Help

For the cash rich, commercial programs like Photoshop or MetaTools Fractal Design Painter are truly excellent ways of creating and retouching your work. But if cash is a problem there are many cheap (and even free) packages which will do the job. Visit:

Windows95.com

http://www. windows95.com

Tucows

http://www.tucows.com

The Ultimate Macintosh

http://www.freepress.com/umac/

For a more immediate start:

PC Paint Packages

http://www.jasc.com/psp.html – PaintShop Pro

http://www.micrografx.com/picturepublisher/ – Picture Publisher

ftp://ftp.arcsoft.com/www/ftp/ps20.exe – Photostudio

PC GIF animation packages

http://rtlsoft.com/animagic/animag32.zip – Animagic

ftp://ftp.mindworkshop.com/pub/alchemy/gifcon32.exe – GifCon 32

http://www.microsoft.com/imagecomposer/gifanimator/ gifanin.htm – Microsoft Gif Animator

Macintosh Paint packages

http://hyperarchive.lcs.mit.edu/HyperArchive/Archive/gst/grf/ painting-111.hqx – painting 1.1

Chapter Four

Tables

Whilst basic HTML is flexible enough to allow simple pages of information to be laid out, there are times when something a little more complex is required. Ideal for tabulating data and expanding page layout, Tables are a powerful tool in the designer's armoury.

Covers

Introduction to Tables

As we have already seen basic HTML carries many tags which are designed to make the layout of text on the page more attractive.

Bold text, colours and differing font sizes can be combined to produce eye-catching effects, but for the display of columnar text and, of course, tabled information there is little that can be done.

Tables, as the name suggests, present a way of presenting data in a highly controlled tabulated form giving greater control over positioning of elements.

In its simplest form a table will allow a designer to fill the middle 80% of the screen with text leaving 10% on either side for white space. At its most complex a table could be used to recreate, say, a periodic table or to show price lists on screen.

With a little careful thought and imaginative usage, tables can become a very important part of any page design.

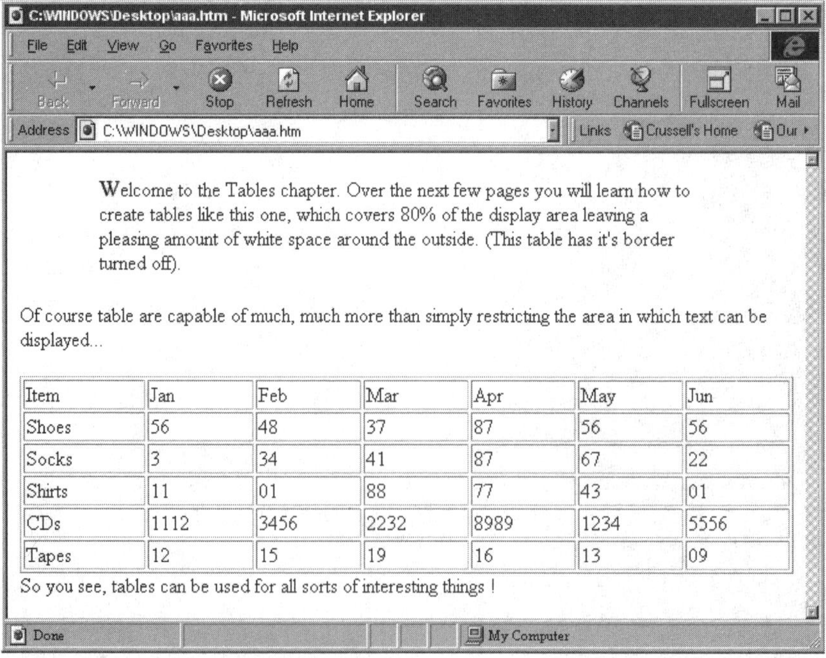

Welcome to the Tables chapter. Over the next few pages you will learn how to create tables like this one, which covers 80% of the display area leaving a pleasing amount of white space around the outside. (This table has it's border turned off).

Of course table are capable of much, much more than simply restricting the area in which text can be displayed...

Item	Jan	Feb	Mar	Apr	May	Jun
Shoes	56	48	37	87	56	56
Socks	3	34	41	87	67	22
Shirts	11	01	88	77	43	01
CDs	1112	3456	2232	8989	1234	5556
Tapes	12	15	19	16	13	09

So you see, tables can be used for all sorts of interesting things !

The <TABLE> tag

The <TABLE> tag is used to signify the start of a table definition. It may contain any or all of the following attributes:

Failing to include a <\TABLE> tag will prevent your table from being displayed in Netscape browsers.

WIDTH

Allows designers to set the width of the table using two methods, either an explicit value or a percentage value. Using the first method it is possible to create a table to exact horizontal dimensions, for example using <TABLE WIDTH=500> would give a table which is fixed to 500 pixels wide.

The second method, whilst not as exact, uses a percentage of the available space which allows the table to expand or contract along with the browser if it is resized at any point. For instance using <TABLE WIDTH=90%> forces the table to take 90% of the available horizontal space.

HEIGHT

Not all browsers will interpret this attribute so care should be used when including it in a table layout.

Those browsers that do accept the HEIGHT attribute will allow designers to set the table height in the same way as its width (see above), allowing the table height to be defined as either an explicit number of pixels or as a percentage of the visible display area.

BORDER

This attribute sets the thickness of the borders surrounding the table.

Setting a value is simply a matter of specifying BORDER=X within the table tag, where x is the desired width in pixels.

If no value is given or BORDER=0 is entered no border will appear.

If the construction <TABLE BORDER> is used a border value of one pixel will be assumed.

Rows and Columns

Every table is a collection of rows and cells. Every row (horizontal 'slice' of the table) contains a number of cells, each of which contain the table information.

Rows must be set up before cells can be added in. In order to create a table row the <TR> and </TR> container pair is used. Each row can contain any number of cells.

Table Rows

The <TR> tag can take up to three attributes:

ALIGN

Specifies the horizontal alignment of cell data for a row. ALIGN can be either LEFT, RIGHT or CENTER.

VALIGN

Specifies the vertical alignment of cell data for a row. It takes one of the values TOP, MIDDLE or BOTTOM.

BGCOLOR

A recent addition to the table attributes, BGCOLOR takes the same values as the BGCOLOR attribute of the BODY tag. Be aware that this attribute is not supported in all browsers.

Table Cells

For every ROW in a table there must be a number of cells which contain the data to be displayed.

Each cell within a row is defined using the <TD> and </TD> or <TH> </TH> container pairs. <TH>, or table header, is used to define a cell which contains a heading.

Text within the <TH> container usually appears centred and in bold to make it stand out.

<TD> (table data) is the most widely used cell tag and simply specifies the start and end tag of a cell which may hold data.

Every <TH> and <TD> can take the following attributes:

CELLSPACING

This attribute sets the size of the 'invisible' margin between individual cells in a table as well as the size of the gap between the cells and the border of the table overall.

CELLPADDING

Cellpadding allows the setting of the gap between the left hand edge of table cells and the start of the cell contents.

Cellpadding can be used to create areas of space within cells so that the cell contents don't appear to be pushed up close to the edge of that cell.

ALIGN

Much like the align attribute used by a number of HTML tags (see chapter 2 for more information), this command allows the horizontal position of the table overall to be set.

Giving values of LEFT and RIGHT allows the table to be pushed against the respective page edge, using CENTER will align the table so it sits neatly in the middle of the page.

VALIGN

As with the attribute of the same name for table rows this allows the designer to specify where the cell contents will physically appear.

BGCOLOR

BGCOLOR allows the background colour of individual cells to be specified. It works in the same way as the BGCOLOR attribute for the BODY tag (see chapter 2).

WIDTH

This attribute allows the width of individual table cells to be specified either as an explicit value or as a percentage of the total table width.

Care should be taken when specifying cell widths as the browser will only allow one width to be used per column.

If multiple widths are specified the browser will resize all cells in that column to the width of the widest.

HEIGHT

Not supported by all browsers, the HEIGHT tag, which can take values explicitly or as percentages, allows the height of table cells to be defined.

As with WIDTH, the browser will try to follow every height value it can, unless it conflicts with other cells in the same row.

If such a conflict occurs the browser will resize all cells in the row to conform to the height of the tallest individual.

NOWRAP

Tells the browser that any text in any cell which uses the NOWRAP attribute must appear as a single line, rather than over a number of lines.

NOWRAP can be useful if a specific sentence is required to fill just one line.

Spanning Rows and Columns

The tags and attributes discussed so far in this chapter have dealt with individual and equal cells in a table.

However tables – like life – are very rarely uniform from start to end.

Sometimes it is desirable to have individual cells which are two, three and more times the size of their peers.

Using the COLSPAN and ROWSPAN attributes it is possible to expand cells but care should be exercised when carrying out such a spanning operation or unpredictable results may occur.

The format of COLSPAN and ROWSPAN is the same, simply insert COLSPAN=X or ROWSPAN=X into a <TD> to activate.

The value X can be anything from 2 to the maximum number of cells in the width or height.

Values greater than the total number have no extra effect but it is best not to exceed the actual total as this may cause problems later on if the table is extended.

Spanned cells always extend to the right of their own position (in the case of a row span) or into the space below their own position (if it's a col span). It is not possible to tell a cell to span into space above or to the left of its own position.

It must also be borne in mind that the span extends the size of the cell to the right or below or both if a <TD> contains ROWSPAN and COLSPAN.

Because of this it is necessary to drop a cell definition in the appropriate direction for each span used in order to make sufficient space for the expanded cell. Failing to do so can lead to problems.

For example, consider the following table definition:

```
<TABLE border=1>
<TR><TD>Row 1, Cell 1</TD><TD>Row 1 Cell 2</TD>
<TD>Row 1 Cell 3</TD>
</TR>
<TR><TD ROWSPAN=2>Row 2, Cell 1</TD>
<TD COLSPAN=2>Row 2 Cell 2</TD>
</TR>
<TR><TD>Row 3 Cell 2</TD><TD>Row 3 Cell 3</TD>
</TR>
</TABLE>
```

Notice that in the second row the first cell contains a ROWSPAN=2 attribute. As this cell will expand downwards it is necessary to include one less cell definition in the third row. The second cell of row 2 contains a colspan=2 attribute which means row 2 requires one less cell as the second cell will also occupy the space the third cell would have used.

The results of the above code are thus:

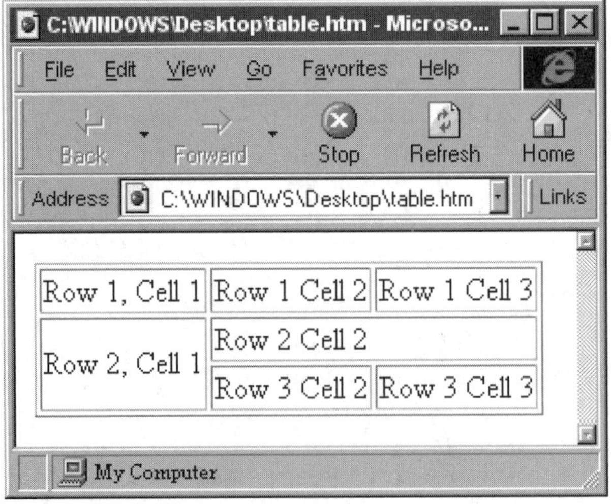

It is important to stress that if you forget to omit the necessary cell definitions to accommodate any spans used 'ghosting' may occur.

Turn table borders ON to help find "ghost" cells.

Ghosting is the unwanted appearance of table cells outside of the expected range.

For example, imagine a table which is designed to have three cells per row. If the second cell of the second row contains a span command which tells it to expand into the space its neighbour should occupy it is essential to remember not to include the cell which should, by rights, occupy the next space. Inclusion of such a cell will create a ghost as the example below illustrates.

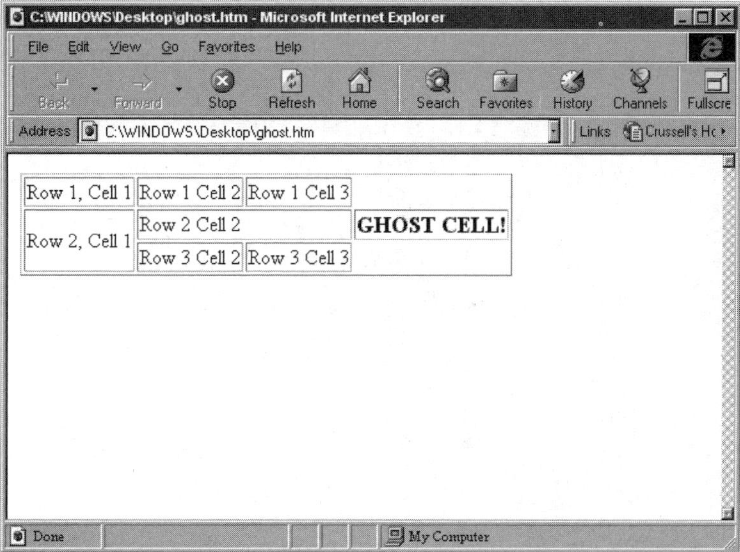

This can be a real annoyance, especially where complicated table designs are involved and care should be taken to ensure this does not happen. The easiest way to spot ghosting is to turn the table border on using BORDER=1 which will allow you to see where the cells should be and easily identify the position of any ghosts.

A Helpful Example

```
<table width=90% border=1>
<caption><font size=+1>Website hits by day of          1
the week</font></caption>

<tr align=left>
<td>W/C</td><td>Mon</td><td>Tue</
td><td>Wed</td><td>Thurs</td><td>Fri</          2
td><td>Sat</td><td>Sun</td></tr>

<tr><td colspan=8><hr></td></tr>          3

<tr align=center>
<td bgcolor="#bfbfbf">24/11</td><td>1000</
td><td>2000</td><td>650</td><td>566</          4
td><td>2500</td><td>2342</td><td>1999
</td></tr>

<tr align=center>
<td bgcolor="#bfbfbf">01/12</td><td>978</
td><td>1234</td><td>999</td><td>1212          5
</td><td>697</td><td>2121</td><td>878
</td></tr>

<tr align=center>
<td bgcolor="#bfbfbf">08/12</td><td>1010</
td><td>2020</td><td>560</td><td>665</          6
td><td>1500
</td><td>2432</td><td>999</td></tr>

</table>          7
```

The breakdown of this code is as follows:

1 The table is defined and is set to take up 90% of the entire displayable width of the browser.

The border thickness is set to one pixel and a caption is defined to sit at the top of the table.

2 Here, the <TR> has been given the attribute ALIGN=LEFT which will force all of the cells in this row to place their contents butted up to the left-hand side.

Eight cells are defined, together with their contents.

3 This row has only one cell which has spanned to fill the width of the table. Because the span is set to eight there is no need to declare any others, this would merely create a set of ghosts (see earlier in the chapter for more details).

This cell has been filled with a <HR> which will place a horizontal line across the table.

4 This row has been set to align all cell contents to center.

Note that the first cell in the row has its own background colour definition which will give a medium grey colour.

5&6 These rows are the same as row 4.

7 A very important table element which closes off the table.

Failure to include this tag in a table definition can cause unpredictable results.

The results of this portion of code can be seen overleaf.

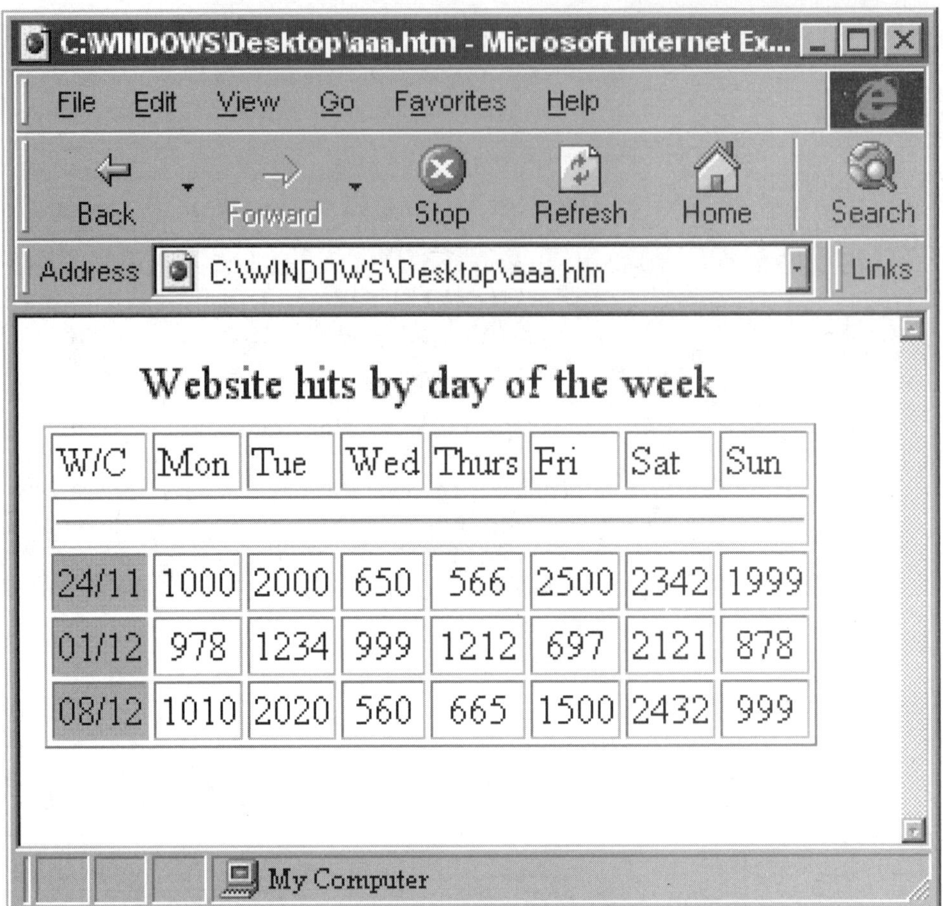

W/C	Mon	Tue	Wed	Thurs	Fri	Sat	Sun
24/11	1000	2000	650	566	2500	2342	1999
01/12	978	1234	999	1212	697	2121	878
08/12	1010	2020	560	665	1500	2432	999

Chapter Five

Frames

There are times when using static pages within a web browser is just not enough. Navigational aids, graphic advertisements and other features may be required onscreen at all times. In order to help achieve this, HTML presents us with a facility called Frames.

Covers

Introduction to Frames

Sometimes it's desirable to keep certain elements of a site design onscreen at all times. A common navigational system, for example, may be required to sit permanently in a space of its own on the left hand side of the screen.

Using standard HTML tags to achieve this would mean coding the same information onto every page where the navigational aid is required – a laborious task on a site of any size! It becomes even more tedious to maintain the site if the navigational aid should change as every page on the site would need updating.

Web browsers from NetScape 2 and upwards made provision for such a situation with the introduction of FRAMES, which in essence allow the browser display area to hold multiple HTML documents at the same time without interfering with one another.

The advantages of such a facility are obvious. As each frame behaves as an independent browser page, it is not affected by its neighbours when the page is changed, unless the designer specifies it that way. This means that the navigational system can be created as a single HTML file and can be made to remain constant throughout a site. Any changes that need to be made to that navigational system now only affect a single file.

However, a small percentage of browsers are not equipped to handle frames, so whatever it is that is contained within any extra frames on the page should be non-essential to the operation of the site, as it won't appear on such browsers.

Be aware from the start that frames can be difficult beasts to deal with and badly designed frames and framesets can be more of a hindrance than a help to those visiting your site.

A few minutes of careful thought and pre-planning can save hours of heartache and complaints from site visitors at a later date.

The <FRAMESET> tag

The <FRAMESET> </FRAMESET> container pair is a major departure from standard HTML as it appears on a page without the prerequisite <BODY> </BODY> and </HTML> tags. <FRAMESET> pages make up the template for what will follow and as such are significantly different.

<FRAMESET> can take the following attributes:

ROWS

A list of values which tells the browser to split the available window area into a given number of horizontal spaces. ROWS will accept three kinds of values: explicit i.e. 50 (pixels), percentage and the '*' value, which is an HTML shorthand for 'the rest of the available space'.

Make sure your rows and colums do not exceed 100% of the display area – otherwise they won't display properly.

COLS

Similar to the ROWS attribute except this value tells the browser to split the display space into vertical areas. COLS accepts the explicit, percentage and '*' values in the same way as ROWS (see above).

It is very important to note that each <FRAMESET> can contain either a row declaration or a COLS but not both. If a page design needs to use a combination of the two a further <FRAMESET> can be embedded.

In setting up a <FRAMESET> declaration it is important to bear size in mind. Perhaps the simplest frames approach utilises just the explicit declaration for frame size, for example:

```
<FRAMESET COLS="400,400">
```

This frameset would effectively split the screen in two creating two frames, each of which are 400 pixels in width.

The problem arises from the actual sizes specified in the declaration. The total screen width required to display both frames in all their glory would be 800 pixels, which is fine for those who have high resolution screens, but leaves those with lower resolution screens out in the dark a little as they cannot fit the whole page on the screen at once.

One way around this is to use the percentage declarations, in much the same way as tables use them (see chapter 4).

Using this approach the previous example could be recoded to read:

```
<FRAMESET COLS="50%,50%">
```

This tells the browser to create two frames which split the displayable area in the middle. As the percentage has been used the two frame areas will automatically resize if the browser window is resized.

There is, of course the final parameter which is the '*'. Suppose the page design calls for a single frame at the left hand edge of the screen which is to be used to display a series of links to other sites and the rest of the displayable area is to display site contents. The links bar needs to be exactly 150 pixels wide, so using the percentage declaration is ruled out and explicit declarations are made impossible because the browser window can be resized.

In order to achieve the desired effect the following code can be employed:

```
<FRAMESET COLS="150,*">
```

This tells the browser to make the first frame 150 pixels wide and to devote the rest of the space to the second frame.

Note that it is possible to use the * parameter anywhere within the FRAMESET declaration i.e. <FRAMESET COLS="*,150"> will create a frame 150 pixels wide at the right hand edge of the browser and devote the rest of the displayable area to what is effectively the first frame.

Frameset Examples

Framesets can be difficult to understand, especially for the beginner.

What follows here are some short examples of what can be achieved using frames together with the code which created them.

Example 1

This example shows how to create a page which is divided horizontally. This type of approach is often used in situations where it is desirable to place some form of page header or advertising banner at the head of the page and have the content appear in the bottom frame. The advantage of this, of course, is that while the contents of the bottom frame may change, the top frame will remain the same.

```
<frameset  rows="25%,75%">
        <frame src="top.html" name="top">
        <frame src="bottom.html" name="bottom">
</frameset>
```

When combined with suitable HTML files for the contents of both frames (top.html and bottom.html) the end result will be:

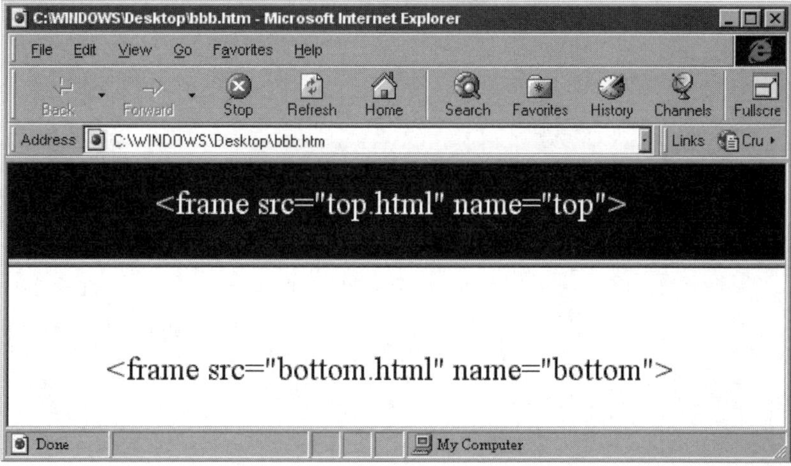

Example 2

In a reversal from Example 1, this sample code creates two frames in a vertical split.

This kind of approach might be used if navigation buttons or a permanent list of some variety is required.

```
<frameset  cols="15%,85%">
      <frame src="left.html" name="left">
      <frame src="right.html" name="right">
</frameset>
```

This code will produce a frames page which looks like this:

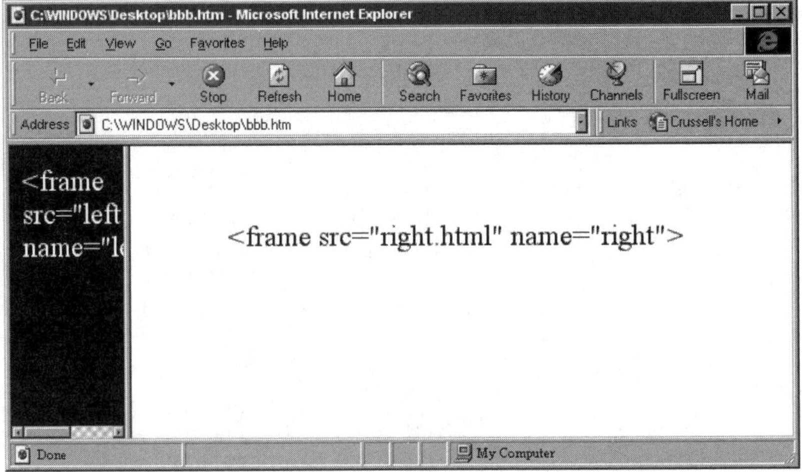

Example 3

This example combines the elements of both previous framesets.

Note that it contains nested frameset commands (one inside the other) which allows the creation of extremely complex page designs.

```
<frameset cols="15%,85%">
      <frame src="left.html" name="left">
      <frameset rows="40%,*">
            <frame src="right1.html" name="right1">
            <frame src="right2.html" name="right2">
      </frameset>
</frameset>
```

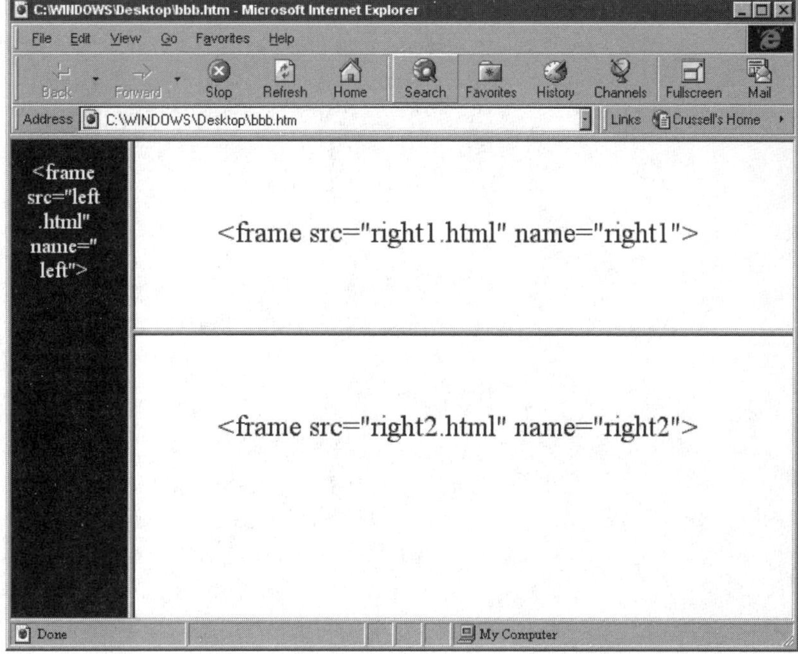

Note how the frameset definition for the frames named right1 and right2 is ‘embedded’ within the outer frameset definition. Using this technique enables us to split the rightmost frame into smaller portions.

Putting the Picture in the FRAME

Once the FRAMESET has been defined it is necessary to tell the browser what to put into each individual FRAME element of the set.

This is achieved using the <FRAME> tag and its associated attributes. For every entry in the FRAMESET there should be a corresponding FRAME declaration.

The FRAME tag takes the following attributes:

SRC

The SRC is the most important of the FRAME attributes as it allows the designer to specify the HTML file which will sit within the frame that is being defined. Remember that the frame itself merely creates what is effectively a browser window within the main browser window and requires some content to fill it.

NAME

Allows a name to be assigned to the current frame. Although this may seem a little pointless at this stage the purpose will be made clear in the next section on the use of the TARGET.

MARGINWIDTH

This attribute specifies the width of the left and right margins for the frame, inserting some space between the edge of the frame and the text or images. In more modern browsers, such as Internet Explorer 3 and Netscape Communicator specifying a value of 0 here will create a 'seamless' look to the frame.

MARGINHEIGHT

Marginheight allows the designer to specify the height of the top and bottom margins for the frame. As with MARGINWIDTH, specifying values of zero will create a 'seamless' look to the frame.

SCROLLING

This attribute takes one of the values YES, NO or AUTO. If YES is selected the frame will be created with scroll bars included as standard, which is helpful if your frame is to include long pages of information.

A value of NO will always omit the scroll bars, so if the page is longer than the displayable area the remaining text will be lost to the viewer.

AUTO leaves the decision making to the browser which will include scroll bars if they are required and omit them otherwise.

NORESIZE

Ordinarily it is possible for the user to manually resize the size of onscreen frames by dragging the frame border markers. If NORESIZE is included in the FRAME declaration the frame size is fixed and cannot be altered. This can be very useful in situations where text and images have been designed for a specific frame width or height and altering the frame dimensions would spoil the look and feel of the page as a whole.

Putting all of these elements together gives us the following:

```
<FRAMESET COLS="100,*">
  <FRAME SRC="leftbar.html" name="navbar"
   MARGINWIDTH=3 MARGINHEIGHT=3 NORESIZE>
  <FRAME SRC="main.html" name="main">
</FRAMESET>
```

The effect of this code is to create a page with two columnar frames, the first 100 pixels wide, the second taking up the rest of the displayable area.

The leftmost frame, named navbar, will call the HTML file called leftbar.html and has left, right, top and bottom margins set to three pixels. It may not be resized as the NORESIZE attribute has been included.

The second frame, named main, takes its content from a file called main.html. Because there are no other attributes set it will assume suitable default values for the MARGINWIDTH and MARGINHEIGHT and it may be resized.

With suitable HTML files created for leftnav and main the result will look like this:

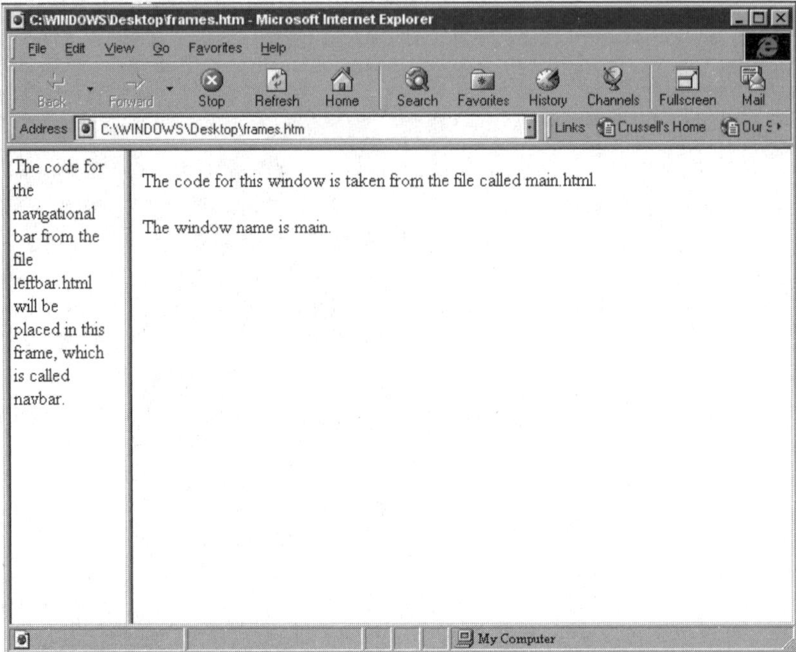

NOFRAMES

Frames are all well and good, but not all browsers support them.

In order to provide for visitors without frames-compatible browsers the <NOFRAMES> container is provided. Within NOFRAMES containers designers can include any standard HTML tags. In some instances this can be sued to provide a frames-free page.

In other circumstances the code within <NOFRAMES> might be a simple message informing visitors that a particular browser is required if viewing is to continue.

The TARGET attribute

Within the bounds of a normal HTML page, clicking on a hyperlink will clear the current contents of the browser and replace it with something fresh.

A frames-based page is a different proposition as each frame can hold an HTML document of its own. Sometimes, for instance with big websites, it is desirable to use one frame as a static index and when one of the links is clicked, to display the selected page in another window.

In order to do this it is necessary to use the TARGET attribute which can be added to the anchor tag.

The TARGET attribute has much greater power however and can be used in a variety of ways as we shall see.

Using TARGET in a hyperlink

By inserting the TARGET attribute into a hyperlink the designer can specify which frame the selected link will be loaded into. Take the case:

```
<a href="page.html" TARGET="mainpane">Click me</a>
```

When the link is clicked the browser will take the page called page.html and put it straight into the frame called mainpane. It is important to note that if the name given in the TARGET attribute does not correspond with the name of an existing frame a whole new browser will be launched to display the page.

Using TARGET in a client-side image map

When using client-side image maps the TARGET attribute can be added to the AREA definitions (see chapter 3) to specify where the selected page will be displayed. For example:

```
...
<AREA SHAPE=RECT COORDS="8,5,147,22"
HREF="happy.html" TARGET="display">
```

Using TARGET in a Form

The TARGET attribute can be used when creating HTML forms.

See the next chapter for more information on forms and using TARGET.

TARGET's special names

As previously explained the TARGET attribute requires a name associated with it to tell the browser where to place new data.

HTML provides four special names for use with TARGET which all begin with the '_' (underscore) character.

_SELF

Using TARGET="_self" tells the browser to place the new data in the same pane as the link that was clicked.

_BLANK

The intriguingly named _blank is used when it is desirable to open a whole new browser window.

_PARENT

Using the _PARENT name forces the browser to go up a level in the frames hierarchy. For example, if a call to _PARENT is made inside a frame, the browser will reference the FRAMESET command that contains the definition for the calling frame.

If the calling frame has no logical parent the call will be treated in the same way as a call to _SELF.

_TOP

Always throws the new content into the whole browser window, removing any frames which were previously created and treating the entire browser displayable area as a single frame pane.

Chapter Six

Forms

From time to time the necessity arises to collect information from a visitor.

Using the wide variety of devices which Forms present, all this becomes a straightforward task.

Covers

Why use a Form?

Basic HTML provides a host of features which allow the designer to define the way in which text and images are to be displayed on a page.

But this simple collection of commands has no way of allowing the website owner to collect information from the visitor.

Such an operation can prove to be very useful – especially if the site is a commercial one – and it's helpful to collect details on visitors who wish to be sent detailed information at a later date.

On a more personal level it may be desirable to collect email addresses of visitors so they may be contacted when the site details are updated.

In order to help collect such information, HTML provides us with a series of features collectively known as form elements.

From text boxes which allow details such as names to be entered to user-defined selections and drop-down boxes, forms provide a highly flexible way to gather the information which can be emailed to a particular individual or sent to a server for more specialised processing.

In this chapter we will examine the various form controls and discuss ways in which the data they gather can be passed on.

The <FORM> tag

This container pair tells the browser that whatever is contained between the <FORM> and </FORM> tags is a set of commands which are designed specifically for the collection of information through a web page which will be passed to the page owner.

The FORM definition may contain a number of attributes which tell the browser exactly what to do with the data once it has been entered. These attributes are:

In order to work properly, forms must be linked to an appropriate CGI script.

ACTION

The action attribute defines which procedure will take place when the data is being sent. Usually ACTION takes one of two values – the URL of a suitable server script which will accept the form data and process it (for more on server scripts see Chapter 11 on CGI) or a mailto: declaration which gives the email address of the recipient of the form information.

METHOD

METHOD defines the way in which the data from the form is physically transmitted over the Internet. The Method accepts one of two attributes:

POST

This approach is the most commonly used and simply sends the form information to the relevant CGI script or email address.

GET

Using the GET attribute forces the browser to pass the form information by appending it to the URL specified in the GET command. Each portion of information is separated from the rest by means of the '?' character.

Whilst there are several situations where this method of sending data is most suited, it can be a tricky beast to deal with for any number of reasons, and so it's probably best to avoid it.

Input tags for Forms

Once the <FORM> definition has been created it is necessary to place some commands within it to accept the desired data.

The <INPUT> tag is used for this purpose and collects data typed from the keyboard. There are a number of other ways to collect information and we shall examine those later in this chapter.

INPUT can take several forms but unlike the <FORM> tag itself is not a container and does not carry a </INPUT> partner tag.

The format of the tag is:

```
<INPUT NAME="aname" TYPE="(see below)">
```

Each input tag should have a unique NAME associated with it. Failing to associate such a name can result in unpredictable results and incorrect data being returned.

The attributes for INPUT are:

TYPE=TEXT

The text type displays an input box which is one line deep. It carries several sub-attributes to define the way in which data will be accepted:

SIZE

The length (in characters) of the input box on-screen.

VALUE

The initial text which will be displayed in the textbox. This is useful if it is necessary to set a default value for a particular textbox.

MAXLENGTH

The maximum length of the input (in characters). This attribute is very useful for instances where only a certain number of characters are required – telephone numbers for instance.

TYPE=PASSWORD

The PASSWORD attribute is identical to its TEXT cousin with the exception that when the user types information into the associated onscreen box a star character '*' is displayed for each ordinary character entered.

This can be useful for providing access to restricted areas of a website or providing special user identification in a form.

TYPE=TEXTAREA

The TEXTAREA expands on the TEXT tag, providing an extended box which allows users to enter data over several lines.

TEXTAREA is a container pair and any normal text between the <TEXTAREA> and </TEXTAREA> will be placed into the on-screen box as the default entry.

Attributes for <TEXTAREA> are:

ROWS

Specified in characters this value tells the browser how many lines high to make the input box. Users can type as many lines of text as they like, but if the number entered exceeds the number specified by ROWS, a scroll bar will appear within the box to indicate the depth of the entry.

COLS

Specified in characters this value tells the browser how wide to make the TEXTAREA. If lines entered by users exceed the value specified by COLS some browsers will provide scrollbars in a similar way to that described above whilst others will simply wrap the text within the TEXTAREA.

In addition to the text entry tags there are also a number of INPUT commands which will allow choices and selections to be made:

TYPE=CHECKBOX

The checkbox type performs a task similar to the multiple selection boxes often found on questionnaires. Checkboxes can be used to allow those filling in the form to select just one item from a list or multiple items.

In its simplest form the CHECKBOX allows users the choice of 'on' or 'off' – useful for including those boxes where visitors can tick a box to request further information or leave it empty if the info is not required.

To produce this type of box use a variant of the following code:

```
<INPUT TYPE=CHECKBOX NAME="moreinfo"
VALUE="sendit">
```

Using this code the checkbox, which is named moreinfo, will send a value of 'sendit' if the user clicks in the box. If the box remains unchecked no value will be sent.

To create a list of multiple items where several can be selected it is necessary to create several instances of the CHECKBOX tag, where each instance contains the same NAME but differing values. This approach allows any of the boxes to be ticked and will send the VALUEs of all those selected when the form is submitted.

The following code segment will produce a multiple selection item:

```
Please send me more information on:
Floppy Disks <INPUT TYPE=CHECKBOX NAME="request"
VALUE="floppy disks">
Hard Disks <INPUT TYPE=CHECKBOX NAME="request"
VALUE="hard disks">
```

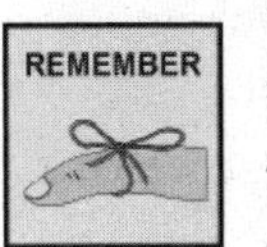

It is important to give each INPUT tag in a multi-select the same NAME.

```
CD ROMS <INPUT TYPE=CHECKBOX NAME="request"
VALUE="CD ROMS">
Zip Disks <INPUT TYPE=CHECKBOX NAME="request"
VALUE="zip disks">
```

Giving one of the CHECKBOX definitions the additional attribute CHECKED=TRUE will display that CHECKBOX with an initial tick (showing it's the default option).

TYPE=RADIO

It is not always desirable to allow multiple selections from a list and sometimes it's better to have them make one, and only one, selection.

The radio button allows us to do this (it's called a radio button as it mimics the operation of push button radios where only one frequency button could be selected).

As with the CHECKBOX, each radio button definition for a selection set should have the same NAME and different VALUEs. Adding CHECKED=TRUE to one of the items in the list will set it as the default.

The following code fragment demonstrates the use of the radio button:

```
Would you like more information?<P>
<INPUT TYPE=RADIO NAME="moreinfo" VALUE="yes"
CHECKED="YES">
<INPUT TYPE=RADIO NAME="moreinfo" VALUE="no">
```

SELECTions

The <SELECT> tag embodies the best parts from the previous two forms of list, allowing one or several selections to be made from a single list.

The SELECT container pair holds a number of instances of the <OPTION> tag – a one line tag which contains a text item.

This text item will appear as part of the list when it is displayed on-screen and also provides the text which will be returned to the server or email address when the form is submitted.

Adding the attribute SELECTED to an OPTION tag will result in the item being highlighted as the default.

If the MULTIPLE attribute is added to the <SELECT> tag visitors may select more than one item from the list which will be displayed in a box with a scrollbar. Omitting MULTIPLE will result in a drop-down box from which only one option can be selected.

The following code fragment illustrates the way in which the SELECT tag is used:

```
What's your favourite colour?<P>
<SELECT>
    <OPTION>Orange
    <OPTION SELECTED>Red
    <OPTION>Yellow
    <OPTION>Purple
    <OPTION>Green
<SELECT>
```

TYPE=HIDDEN

Just to prove that every conceivable situation has been catered for, HTML provides us with the HIDDEN type, which is invisible to the user and cannot be changed by on-screen input.

The major use for hidden values comes when forms are combined with CGI scripts (see Chapter 11).

Because of the way HTML, Forms and World Wide Web servers communicate it is often impossible to detect if Forms have been filled completed in a particular way.

By combining HIDDEN data with CGI scripts it is possible to track such information and even to introduce new, hidden information which allows the way the forms appear and control to be dictated.

TYPE=SUBMIT and TYPE=RESET

These two types mark the final elements in a <FORM> which allow the user, once data has been entered, to either send it or to clear it completely and re-start.

The buttons take the format:

```
<INPUT TYPE=SUBMIT VALUE="Enter details">
<INPUT TYPE=RESET VALUE="Start again">
```

The VALUE attribute determines what text will appear on each button.

In order to make the SUBMIT button more attractive it is possible to use TYPE=IMAGE in its place. It does the same job – when it's clicked it sends the form data – but it allows a graphic image to be used in place of the rather drab grey button SUBMIT presents us with. An example of this tag is:

```
<INPUT TYPE="IMAGE" SRC="mygrafic.gif" ALIGN="LEFT">
```

Forms – An Example

```
<FORM METHOD="POST"
ACTION="mailto:crussell@ukonline.co.uk">
   Please enter your details:<P>

   Name: <INPUT TYPE="text" SIZE="40"                    1
NAME="name">

<p>
   Address: <TEXTAREA NAME="address" ROWS="3"            2
COLS="40"></TEXTAREA>
<p>

Age: 0-10<INPUT TYPE="radio" checked NAME="age"
value="0-10">
      11-20<INPUT TYPE="radio" NAME="age"                3
value="11-20">
      21-30<INPUT TYPE="radio" NAME="age"
   value="21-30">
      31-40<INPUT TYPE="radio" NAME="age"
   value="31-40">
      41-50<INPUT TYPE="radio" NAME="age"
   value="41-50">

<p>
 Your Interests:<br>
   <INPUT TYPE="checkbox" NAME="Interests"
VALUE="Gardening">Gardening<br>                          4
   <INPUT TYPE="checkbox" NAME="Interests"
VALUE="Motoring">Motoring<br>
   <INPUT TYPE="checkbox" NAME="Interests"
VALUE="Computing">Computing<br>
```

```
<BR>
   Your earnings
      <SELECT NAME="earnings" size="1">
      <OPTION>£0-5,000
      <OPTION>£5,001-£10,000                                5
      <OPTION>£10,001-£20,000
      <OPTION>£20,001-£30,000
      <OPTION>£30,001-£40,000
</SELECT><p>
<INPUT TYPE="submit" name="Submit"                          6
value="Submit">
<INPUT TYPE="reset" name="Reset Form"
value="Reset">
```

The form works in the following way:

1. Creates a single-line textbox 40 characters wide which will accept the users name.
2. A multi-line textbox 40 characters wide by 3 lines high which will accept the users address.
3. This radio button set allows the user to define his or her age. Note that the first box (0-11 years) contains the attribute CHECKED which represents the default value.
4. Checkboxes which allow the user to select several interest areas.
5. A SELECTion which presents a drop-down box from which the user can select only one value. If the <SELECT> tag had contained the MULTIPLE attribute several values could have been selected.

6 The SUBMIT and RESET buttons are defined here. Failing to include these will render the form useless as there's no way to tell the browser when the form-filling has been completed.

When the page is accessed it will look like this:

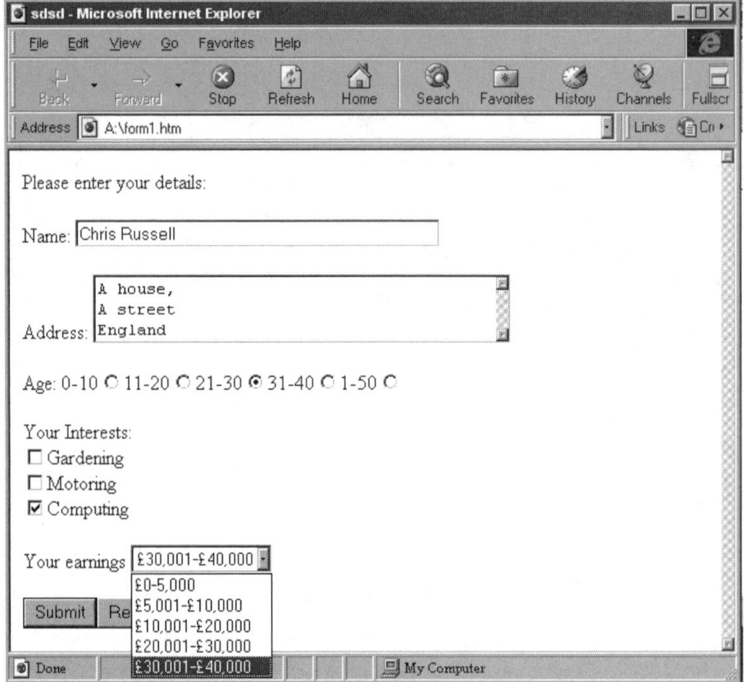

Chapter Seven

Adding Sound and Video

There's a lot more to the web than standard HTML and one way to add more impact to a site is to include sound and video.

In this chapter we'll look at the options available to the page designer and the ways in which they can be implemented.

Covers

Sound and Video formats

As web designers look beyond the boundaries of basic HTML, the next logical step in creating a compelling experience for site visitors is to turn to audio and video.

Moving images and well placed sounds can really make a website stand out from its peers and with a little work can complement the static text content of a page.

Sound for the web comes in two main formats, digital audio or WAV and synthesised music or MIDI format. Both types of file are compatible with all browsers making them the frontrunners in the web music battle, although there are many other formats which may be used if desired.

WAV is a very versatile Microsoft Windows format which allows anything from music samples to voices to be digitally recorded for later playback, either from a sound player or over the web.

The MIDI format cannot handle digital data and instead draws on collections of preset musical sounds which are usually stored on a chip on your PC sound card.

Similarly there are two main video formats, AVI (Audio Video Interleave) and QT (Quicktime) which are used for the majority of video material displayed on the web.

AVI is the Windows format for video storage whilst QT was developed by Apple for displaying moving pictures on their successful range of Macintosh computers. These days however it's common to find players for both types of file on all machines making them easily interchangeable.

Occasionally a new feature comes along which changes our view of the web, and at the moment the big favourite is streamed audio and video. Streaming content over the web is a complex exercise which we will look at in a little more detail later in this chapter. If you can afford to do it however, it can really make a splash!

Adding Sounds to a Page

Adding sounds to any page is quite a straightforward affair relying on the <A> tag.

In order to place a sound or video to a page simply create a hyperlink which points to it. For example:

```
<a href="mysound.wav">Click here for my sound</a>
```

or

```
<a href="mysound.avi">Click here to see my video</a>
```

Short sounds are better than long ones – especially for those downloading your webpages!

When the user clicks the hyperlink the browser will automatically launch a suitable player if one exists. If not, the browser will ask if you wish to save the file to disk.

Whilst sound and videos are great things to include in web pages, care should be taken that the files being used are of a reasonable size.

Short digital sounds or film segments of just a few seconds are all well and good, but placing a 60 megabyte feature film of a family wedding can only infuriate the casual visitor who may have to wait an awfully long time to download and view something they have little interest in.

Unless you have the ability to stream information (see later this chapter) the key to success is to keep it short, unless you know in advance that the people visiting your site are likely to have extremely fast modem connections to the Internet.

Background Sounds

Perhaps the easiest way to add sounds to a page is to use the <BGSOUND> tag.

It sounds easy to do, and in effect it is. But only if you happen to be running Microsoft's Internet Explorer.

The <BGSOUND> tag can sit anywhere in an HTML page but for the sake of simplicity it's best to place it in the <HEAD> portion of the document.

<BGSOUND> takes two attributes which will allow the designer to specify the source file to be played and the manner in which it is to be played:

SRC

The SRC attribute allows the designer to specify which sound file is to be played, and where to find it.

LOOP

This attribute takes one of two values, INFINITE which means the sound will continue to play forever and X, where X is any value which determines how many times the sound will play before ending.

Putting it all together gives:

```
<BGSOUND SRC="mysound.wav" LOOP=50>
```

which will play the file called mysound.wav 50 times before ending.

It is worth mentioning that even if a sound is set to play forever it will only continue until such time as the visitor selects a hyperlink and loads a new page into the browser. The only way to make the sound play throughout a site would be to place it in a frame (see chapter 5) which never changes.

At present Netscape doesn't support the <BGSOUND> tag. Take heart then there is an alternative way to include sounds, as well as video, in your web masterpiece.

EMBEDding Content in Web Pages

From Netscape Navigator 2.0 the <EMBED> tag has been made available to allow content and plug-in applications to be included in a web page.

Plug-ins will be covered in the next chapter so, for the time being, we'll concentrate on how to use the <EMBED> tag to place background sounds in an HTML page.

The <EMBED> tag is a more flexible method of introducing sounds than <BGSOUND> because it works in all browsers from Netscape 2.0 upwards.

Attributes for <EMBED> include:

SRC

The SRC attribute allows the designer to specify which sound file should be played.

WIDTH

Allows the width of the sound playing control to be specified. Most sound controls have a small number of buttons including play, rewind and stop associated with them and by specifying the width and height (see below) it is possible to fix the size of the control and buttons.

HEIGHT

Specifies the height of the sound playing control.

HIDDEN

Takes the vales "YES" and "NO". Hides the sound playing control from view – useful in conjuction with AUTOPLAY.

AUTOPLAY

Forces the file specified in SRC to play as soon as it is loaded.

LOOP

Takes the values TRUE or FALSE. Using TRUE forces the browser to endlessly repeat the sound file.

VOLUME

Entering a percentage value between zero and 100 forces the sound tool to alter the playback volume of the sound to the specified level.

Placing it in a page is as simple as:

```
<EMBED SRC="mysound.wav" WIDTH="150" HEIGHT="250"
CONTROLS="TRUE" LOOP="TRUE">
```

This would play back the file mysound.wav, placing the sound player in an area 150 by 250 pixels. The controls for the player would be displayed and the sound will loop. As AUTOPLAY is not set the page visitor would have to use the player controls to start the sound.

```
<EMBED SRC="moresound.wav"  HIDDEN="TRUE"
LOOP="FALSE" VOLUME="50%" AUTOPLAY="YES">
```

The above example will hide the sound player, automatically starting the sound as soon as it is loaded. The sound itself will play once (LOOP is set to FALSE) at half of the maximum possible volume.

By replacing moresound.wav with a movie file it is also possible to EMBED video files in a webpage.

Streaming Audio and Video

As Internet access devices become faster and more efficient the Web has seen a move towards streamed content.

Streaming technologies work in a similar way to television as, unlike standard content which is downloaded once and doesn't change, it is 'broadcast' in real time like a TV picture.

The advantage of such a technique is that there are no long waits for very large files like video clips and long audio messages.

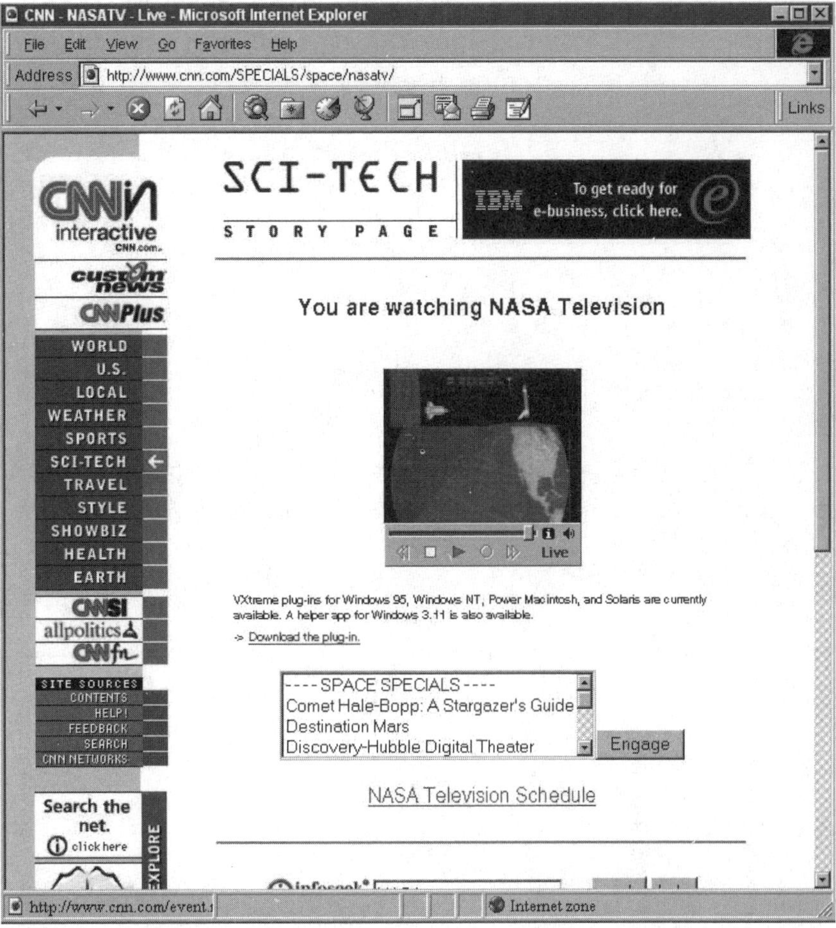

Instead, special software is used within the browser to gather a small portion of the file which is then played as the next portion is downloaded. In this way the illusion is given of the file being constantly played when in effect only a small part of it is held in the computer's memory at any given time.

The disadvantage, of course, is that each time the file is accessed it has to be reloaded from the server on which it sits.

There are a growing number of ways in which content can be played over the Web and both Microsoft and Netscape include special streaming video and audio players with their browser packages in the form of Netshow (http://www.microsoft.com/netshow) and Netcaster (http://developer.netscape.com/one/netcaster/index.html).

Other than these packages perhaps the most popular method of receiving streaming video is through Progressive Networks RealPlayer software (http://www.real.com).

RealPlayer is part of Progressive's RealMedia suite which is dedicated to the creation of files to be played over the Internet.

The process is a complicated and potentially very expensive one so be warned, this is not something for the fainthearted!

Chapter Eight

Active Content

As the web has advanced there have been a constant stream of add-ons and plug-in components made available which fit into the browser allowing it to display non-static, or dynamic, content. In this chapter we will examine some of the technologies available.

Covers

Server Push and Client Pull

One of the oldest techniques for producing 'active content' is known as server push, a procedure where the web server sends a stream of information to the visitor's browser without the need for requests from the browser.

Not all web space providers support server push technologies – remember to check before designing entire sites around server push.

In operation this works in a similar way to very, very simple TV. Where TV transmitters broadcast a series of still images which when updated quickly appear to form a continuous stream, server push sends a series of web pages which are picked up and displayed at specified intervals.

Using server push today is problematic as it relies on the designer being able to turn his or her hand to a number of disciplines, including the creation of CGI code (more on CGI in chapter 11) which can 'push' the content from the server. Push technology is also a very server intensive operation and many web space providers forbid its use as it can tie up huge amounts of system resources.

By far the more palatable approach is client pull, which involves a stream of automatic requests to the server from the client browser, rather than relying on the server to mindlessly pump data out.

Examples of client pull are all over the web, the most common example being used where a designer may want to display some information, a copyright notice for example, for a few seconds before throwing the visitor straight into her, or his, website.

The way to achieve client pull is through the use of the <HTTP META-EQUIV> tag.

Every HTML page has a special identifier attached to it which ensures the browser displays it as HTML and not as a plain text file or a graphic.

This header must conform to the HTTP (HyperText Transfer Protocol) standard which can pass many items of information to the browser, but which is invisible to the person viewing the file.

...contd

In order to force the browser into loading a new page after a given amount of time the following code, inserted into the document head, can be used:

```
<HTTP META-EQUIV="Refresh" CONTENT=10
URL="http://www.computerstep.com">
```

This code tells the browser to execute a REFRESH command (which updates the contents of the browser window) after 10 seconds by loading the page held at http://www.computerstep.com.

Such code has many uses, including the ability to emulate a slideshow, where the viewer can be presented with a series of pages containing images which change every given number of seconds.

It is important to note that when using the refresh, the value of the CONTENT attribute does not take into account time taken to download images or other page information from the server. This can lead to situations where the browser will refresh after the specified time, irrespective of whether or not the page has finished loading.

Also important is that the value held in the URL attribute needs to be a full web address for the desired file. Simply using nextfile.html is not adequate, http://www.me.here.com /nextfile.html is required for the refresh to function correctly in all browsers.

Finally it should be pointed out that it is not possible to supply the <META HTTP-EQUIV> with a list of pages to load one after the other. If a chain of pages is to be displayed each one must contain its own <META HTTP-EQUIV> tag which points to the next page in the sequence.

Browser Plug-ins

The next step up from the rather primitive approach of the client pull is the browser plug-in.

As the Netscape and Microsoft browsers have developed over the last few years, a number of third party companies have sprung up to produce special applications which slot seamlessly into the browser.

There are plug-ins which will carry out all manner of tasks from taking text from a webpage and turning it into digital speech to the highly successful Shockwave plug-in which will display files created with Macromedia's Director package.

The plug-in players are most often given away free by their manufacturers allowing anyone to see content created with their packages.

Plug-in players are placed into an HTML page using the <EMBED> tag which was explained in the last chapter.

Using plug-ins can help to enrich a webpage but it is important to remember that if a visitor doesn't have a particular plug-in installed on their browser they won't be able to see the exciting content.

One way around this is to always include a link to a site where a particular plug-in can be downloaded, so the visitor can install said plug-in on their computer if desired.

For more information on plug-ins take a trip to:

http://www.browser.com

Java and the <APPLET> tag

There's a whole host of free java applets available at http://www.developer.com

Although it seems to be tied to the Internet, the Java programming language was designed to be a next generation discipline to be used on the new breed of Network Computers (or NCs).

The idea behind the NC, which originated from the computer company ORACLE, was to give anyone the ability to purchase a computer at little cost and gain access to any software they required over the Internet. That software is written in Java, a language which was designed to work cross-platform, on any computer which could understand its basic instructions.

The idea was that programmers could write their code in Java and translate it into a common form which could then be used by any Java-capable computer.

The creators of the language, computer giants Sun, based it around the highly popular C language making it accessible to a large percentage of the professional computer programming community. For the beginner however, learning Java can be a highly complex task. The rewards, in terms of what can be achieved once it is understood, can be huge.

There is an ever growing number of programs and instruction manuals available relating to the language and it is way beyond the scope of this book to teach its theory and practice. For those who would like to know more visit:

http://www.developer.com

It is important to note that pure Java programs will not run in a web browser, instead a special type of Java program, known as an applet, is used.

There have been many scare stories around the Internet concerning the security aspects of Java, but as time wears on the minimal chances of anyone exploiting Java applets to damage anyone's PC are getting smaller and smaller.

Placing a Java applet in a web page requires the use of the <APPLET> container.

In addition to a number of attributes listed below which set out the placement information, the <APPLET> may also contain a number of <PARAM> tags, which pass information to the applet before it runs. Standard HTML tags may also be included which will be displayed if the user does not have a Java-enabled browser or if they have Java support turned off.

The attributes for the <APPLET> container are:

NAME

Allows the applet to be given a name. This is useful if several Java applets on the same HTML page need to exchange information.

CODEBASE

Defines the URL of the server directory in which the Java applet code resides. If CODEBASE is not used the browser will look automatically at the directory the page containing the applet came from as the default.

CODE

This attribute contains the name of the Java applet itself. It must contain only the filename and **NOT** the address of the server.

ALT

Like the ALT attribute of the <IMG> tag this allows the designer to include a short sentence of text which will appear if the browser is Java-compatible but for some reason cannot execute the Java code.

WIDTH

Allows the designer to specify how wide the applet will be within the browser.

HEIGHT

Allows the designer to specify how high the applet will be within the browser.

VSPACE

Allows the designer to specify how much 'white space' to place between the top and bottom edges of the applet and the surrounding HTML elements.

HSPACE

Allows the designer to specify how much 'white space' to place between the right and left edges of the applet and the surrounding HTML elements.

<PARAM> is not a container and has only two attributes – NAME and CONTENT. Any number of <PARAM>'s can be included but only those the Java applet is expecting will be accepted, the rest will be simply ignored.

Putting it all together gives us:

```
<applet code="App.class" id="App" width=99 height=99>
   <param name=image value="dusk.gif">
   <param name=millenium value="2000">
   <param name=colour value="Red">
</applet>
```

Note how the <APPLET> tag tells the browser to load App.class, which has an identifier of App and is 99 x 99 pixels within the browser window. As the CODEBASE attribute has not been defined the browser will look for App.class in the same server directory as the one this file came from.

Following the <APPLET> definition are three <PARAM> values which pass details to the java applet – the purpose and function of the <PARAM> contents will vary from applet to applet, but in the case of an applet which scrolls some text up the screen, one of the params may be the text that is to be scrolled, another may be its size and a third its colour.

JavaScript and VBScript

With the release of Navigator 2, NetScape introduced a method of scripting into HTML with its implementation of JavaScript.

JavaScript can be thought of as a cut-down version of Java which is vastly simplified and it can be picked up with ease.

This scripting language has all of the web functionality of its big brother, but the more complex parts have been left out and the remainder adjusted to ensure maximum useability on the web.

Not to be outdone, Microsoft released its own scripting language in the form of VBScript, a web-friendly version of the highly successful Visual Basic. As the name suggests VBScript adheres very closely to the BASIC programming language but in essence does the same job as JavaScript. Of the two JavaScript is the more widely used and has been adopted as netwide standard for scripting, being included as part of the basic design of all modern browsers. As it is the standard we shall use it for the examples given here.

There are two ways to include script within an HTML page. The first is to include it with the <SCRIPT> and </SCRIPT> containers, usually to be found in the <HEAD> of an HTML page.

<SCRIPT> takes two attributes:

LANGUAGE

The LANGUAGE attribute tells the browser which scripting language is being used. For example <SCRIPT LANGUAGE="JavaScript"> or <SCRIPT LANGUAGE="VBScript">

SRC

The SRC attribute points the browser to the location of the script to be used. This can be useful if it is undesirable to place the required scripting code directly into the HTML page.

The second way to place script code into an HTML page is to add it directly into an <A> tag.

This can be very handy in certain situations. For example if it is necessary to build a 'back' button into an HTML page to take the visitor back to the page they just came from we could use the following code:

```
<a href="javascript:history.back()">Click me to go back a page</a>
```

Notice how the usual http://.... information has been replaced by the Javascript command history.back() which tells the browser to flip back a page. There are, of course, many other ways to send the user back, this is just one example of how it might be done using JavaScript.

One of the beauties of JavaScript is its ability to attach handler code to events in HTML pages. Events occur in a number of instances. For example when the user moves the mouse over a hyperlink, chooses to submit a form or to click in a textbox or on a radio button.

When such an event occurs, the browser can be sent off to carry out a task which has been coded in JavaScript. For example if a visitor fills in an HTML form and then clicks the SUBMIT button JavaScript can be used to check that all of the fields in the form have been completed before further action is taken.

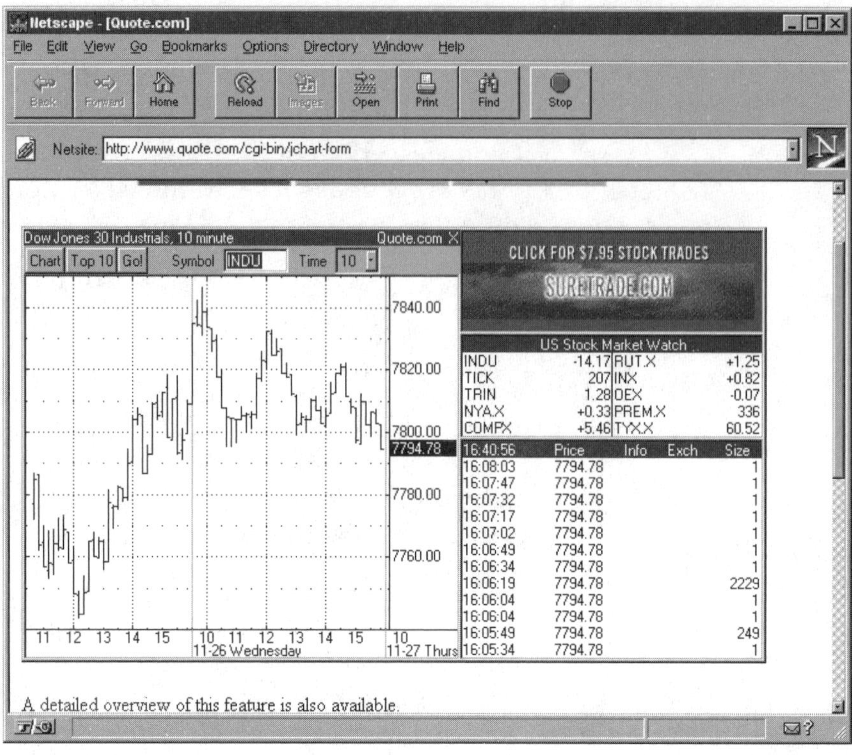

This page is an excellent example of how a Java applet can be used to spice up a webpage.

This particular applet, which refreshes every few minutes, provides regular updates from the American Dow Jones stock exchange.

ActiveX

With the introduction of Internet Explorer 3, Microsoft increased the scope of what was possible within an HTML page through the use of ActiveX components.

ActiveX behaves like a hybrid version of a plug-in crossed with a Java applet, allowing complex programming techniques to be executed. If the browser requires the use of an ActiveX control and the required control is not present on the client machine it is simply downloaded from the web, automatically installed and executed with little or no interruption from the user.

A plus point for ActiveX is its ability to use Microsoft's OLE (Object Linking and Embedding) technology. OLE has been implemented throughout a wide range of Windows-based products and any compatible software program which sports the OLE logo can be used as an effective ActiveX control. What this means is that, for example, Microsoft Word documents can be embedded within an HTML page and will display in an appropriate way.

The ability to display ActiveX controls is not restricted to Microsoft products as a plug-in exists for Netscape which will inform the browser to correctly operate and display suitable controls.

For the more adventurous, Microsoft provide a free program called the ActiveX Control Pad which allows designers to create their own controls for inclusion in web pages.

However, as with the majority of high-end web tools, ActiveX can be a very complex beast and not easy to master. Luckily, Microsoft provide pointers to a number of free controls which can be included in any page.

For the latest on ActiveX visit Microsoft at:

http://www.microsoft.com/activex/controls

Further Information

Active content, the concepts which surround it and the procedures involved in implementing it, could fill a book on its own.

For those keen to find out more, try some of the resources listed below.

Browser plug-ins

http://www.browser.com
All the latest plug-ins as they are released

Java resources

http://reality.sgi.com/employees/shiffman_engr/Java-QA.html
Making sense of Java

http://java.wiwi.uni-frankfurt.de/
The Java repository

ActiveX

http://www.activex.com
One of the largest sources of information relating to ActiveX on the web

http://www.jumbo.com/pages/activex/index.htp
Jumbo.com, free and shareware ActiveX elements for you to use

Chapter Nine

Cascading Style Sheets

So far we've looked at the basics of HTML and discovered how to create page designs, which commands to use for the correct layout of text and images and how to add sounds and other multimedia elements.

This chapter takes a look at the latest developments in HTML, starting with a run down of a new way to place text and images on the page in the form of Cascading Style Sheets.

Covers

Introduction

With the introduction of Internet Explorer 3 in mid-1996 Microsoft introduced a new set of extensions to HTML which expanded the way in which it was possible to lay out text and images within a page.

The extensions, known as Cascading Style Sheets or CSS for short, were adopted by the W3C and included as part of the official HTML standard.

Previously, HTML tags allowed only very cursory positioning abilities – limited to the inclusion of a handful of text sizes, some colours and font faces – CSS created the ability to position text with pixel precision, create custom margins for all or part of a page and even turn off the underlining found on hyperlinks.

Rather than introducing new tags, CSS relies on adding many new attributes to HTML.

The advantage of this approach is that older browsers will simply ignore the new introductions, so whilst the look of the page will not be as effective as it is with more up-to-date browsers it is still possible to view the content.

Starting out with CSS

For the low down on CSS visit: http:// www.cnet.com/ Content/Builder/ Authoring/CSS/ index.html

As already described, Cascading Style Sheets allow the designer a greater degree of control over individual portions of text and images within an HTML page.

Additionally it also allows for the definition of one standard set of styles in a style sheet which can be applied over any number of web pages – for instance it is possible using CSS to create a special definition for page headings which can be called from any page the designer requires.

This definition can be altered at any time within the style sheet and the change will be reflected across every page on which it appears without the need to physically edit and change every one of those pages.

Format of CSS extensions

All CSS definitions, or selectors as they are known, follow a standard format:

```
TAGNAME {property-to-alter: value}
```

Using this is a practical application gives us:

```
P { color: red}
```

The effect of this odd looking command is to tell any browser which supports CSS that for every paragraph of text which starts with the <P> tag and ends with </P> the text is to be set in the colour red. We could of course have included code in the relevant page(s) which simply embedded a <FONT COLOR="RED"> tag into every paragraph but, what if it was decided to change the text colour to green at a later date? Every <FONT COLOR...> tag would have to be altered by hand. Using CSS the definition is required only once and will be applied from that point onwards.

Using this selector definition it's possible to specify similar values to multiple tags. For example:

```
P, H1, H2 {color : #00ff00}
```

sets the colour of all text in a paragraph, H1 and H2 heading to the colour green.

It's also possible to group several definitions together into a single selector:

```
P{color: yellow; font-size: 28pt; font-family: arial}
```

This sets all text between <P> and </P> tags to be yellow in colour, in a type size of 28 points and in the font arial.

If the arial font does not exist the browser default font will be used instead.

Inheriting Styles

Using inheritance it is possible to produce all manner of effects without the need for specifying values for every single tag.

Inheritance works on the basis that once a container tag is opened its effect remains in place until the close tag is included in the HTML.

In the example:

```
<FONT COLOR="red">blah <B>bold bit</B> blah </
FONT>
```

The text will remain red throughout – even where the bold tag is introduced – until the </FONT> appears.

If the <B> tag had been defined as part of the style sheet as being blue (B : {color=blue}) then this would have superseded the command to change the font color to red and the words 'bold bit' would appear in blue.

Inheritance can be a valuable tool as values can even be set relative to those which are already in effect. For example if an HTML page contains the selectors:

```
p {font-size: 14pt};
b {font-size: 200%};
```

and we use the following code:

```
<p>This should be in 14pt <b> and this should be bold and
200% of the original</b></p>
```

The end result will set the standard font size for all the text between <P> and </P> to 14 point. When the browser gets to the bold tag it knows that in addition to carrying out the emboldening operation it must also increase the font size to 200% of what came immediately before. This increase remains in effect until the </b> is encountered when the font size returns to the state it was in before the change (in this case 14pt).

As we have seen it is possible to define a style for a bold tag and, say, a paragraph tag. If the bold tag is used within a paragraph – as in the example above – the paragraph style will be applied in addition to any styles given to the bold tag, provided the styles don't clash in which case the bold would come out on top.

By defining a style for a combination of the two it's possible to add further variety to your style sheets.

For example:

p : {font-family: "jurassic"; font-size : 60pt}

Sets all text in bold in a paragraph to 60pt Jurassic. This effect will only come into play if the browser encounters a bold container pair in a paragraph. A paragraph or a bold tag on its own is not sufficient to involve this text effect.

Putting the Style into HTML

Not everyone has a browser which supports style sheets so do not rely on CSS to position and display important elements in your pages if you want your site to be accessible by everyone.

Once it has been decided which styles are to be used the next step is to place the style information into the relevant documents. There are three ways in which this can be achieved and it's important to decide early on how you intend to do it.

LINKing

Using the <LINK> tag allows the designer to create a file separate from the HTML document which contains all of the style information. These styles can then be linked to documents requiring the style set using the <LINK> tag in the form:

```
<LINK REL=STYLESHEET TYPE="text/css" HREF="http://
my.server.com/mystyle" TITLE="mystyles">
```

This tells the browser to expect a stylesheet called mystyle which can be retrieved from my.server.com.

Using the STYLE tag

To specify the styles for a single HTML document the <STYLE> container pair is used.

Placed in the header, entries between <STYLE> and </STYLE> only apply to the document which contains them.

It is also important to note that older browsers will ignore the <STYLE> tag and display the style definitions as if they were standard text. In order to avoid this the style definitions should be surrounded with comment tags to ensure the older browsers will ignore them. For example:

```
<STYLE>
<!-- older browsers will ignore everything from here ...
      P {color: red}
      B {color: green}
      ADDRESS {color: blue}
older browsers start taking notice again from here -->
</STYLE>
```

The obvious disadvantage of using <STYLE> in every document is that it is time-consuming to update if something changes and increases the size of individual files increasing the download times.

@IMPORT

In order to eliminate the disadvantages of defining full <STYLE> definitions the @IMPORT tag can be used.

This tag will automatically download and insert the style information in an HTML page. The format for this tag is:

```
<STYLE>
<@IMPORT URL("http://my.server.com/style.css")>
```

The above methods of including styles within HTML are all well and good, but the information they contain will be applied to all instances within a page. If a style is defined for the <P> tag it will be applied to all instances of the <P> tag without exception.

Fortunately CSS provides a way of applying 'one-off' effects by allowing styles to be defined within the HTML page and within specific tags.

If, for example, we have a general style set for paragraphs which sets the font to arial and the colour to green but for one particular paragraph it is desirable to set the font to jurassic and the colour to red the following can be included within the HTML document:

```
<P STYLE="FONT-FAMILY:jurassic; COLOR=green">
```

For the scope of this <P> tag the jurassic font in green will be used in preference to any other style which may have been set. Any other paragraphs on the page which do not have styles specifically associated with them will adopt the general style for the <P> tag.

In order to provide even greater control through CSS, it is possible to define classes of data which will allow subsets of previously defined styles to be used and allow the class to be used with any tag and not just under certain circumstances as we have seen previously.

For example, a situation may arise where several different elements within the page are required to be shown in blue text at size 14 points – all bold and italic tags for instance.

The long way around this situation would be to define similar style definitions for both the bold and italic tags. Using classes however, we can set up the definition once and use it wherever necessary within the HTML document.

The class definition for this situation would be:

```
.blue14 {font-color : blue; font-size : 14pt}
```

Notice the period (full-stop) before the class name which identifies this as a class definition and not just an ordinary style definition.

To use this within the page is simply a matter of adding the CLASS attribute to the required HTML tag. It's important to understand that these class definitions will only apply where the CLASS attribute is used –

```
Ordinary text <b>bold text (no class attribute used</b>
more text<b class="blue14">this text will appear in the style
defined by blue14</b>now back to normal
```

Classes can also be used to create subsets of existing styles. The subsets will retain all the properties of their parent style definitions with the exception of anything that is re-defined in the class subset.

If we have a parent style definition:

```
H2    {font-family: "arial";
       font-size: 16pt;
       font-color: green}
```

It is possible to create a subset of the H2 definition which differs, if only slightly:

```
H2.nfont {font-family: "times"}
```

The style definition H2.nfont will inherit the parent properties for font-size and font-color but will take on the new fontstyle times.

Using the definitions within the HTML tags is simply a case of declaring which class you wish to use:

```
<H2>This text appears in 16pt, green, arial</H2>
<H2 class="nfont">This appears in 16pt, green, times</H2>
```

Stylesheets are a very neat, convenient way of spicing up any webpage, but as with all of the more advanced HTML tags and extensions it is very easy to overuse them.

Whilst it may seem like a good idea to have electric pink links in exotic fontfaces in 56 point text, your visitors are sure to grow fed up with them very quickly. Styles should be used sparingly, where the situation requires them rather than everywhere 'because I can'.

Cascading Style Sheets - An Example

```
<head>
<style>
<!--
      P {font-size: 19pt; font-family: "arial"}
      P.smaller {font-size: 14pt;}
      A {text-decoration: none; color: green}
-->
</STYLE>
</HEAD>

<BODY>
This text is displayed in the default font, default style and default
colour.<br><br>

<P>Time for a little action! This text has been enclosed in the
paragraph container pair which has been set to render the
contents in the Arial face at size 19 points</p>

<P class="smaller">And this paragraph has been marked with
the 'smaller' class which is set to size 14 point but which picks up
the Arial font face of it's parent.</p>

<a href="somepage.html">The text to the end of this sentence
is a hyperlink</a>. It has been set to colour green (which is
difficult to see in this black and white image) but has no underline
attached as we have used text-decoration to turn it off.
</BODY>
</HTML>
```

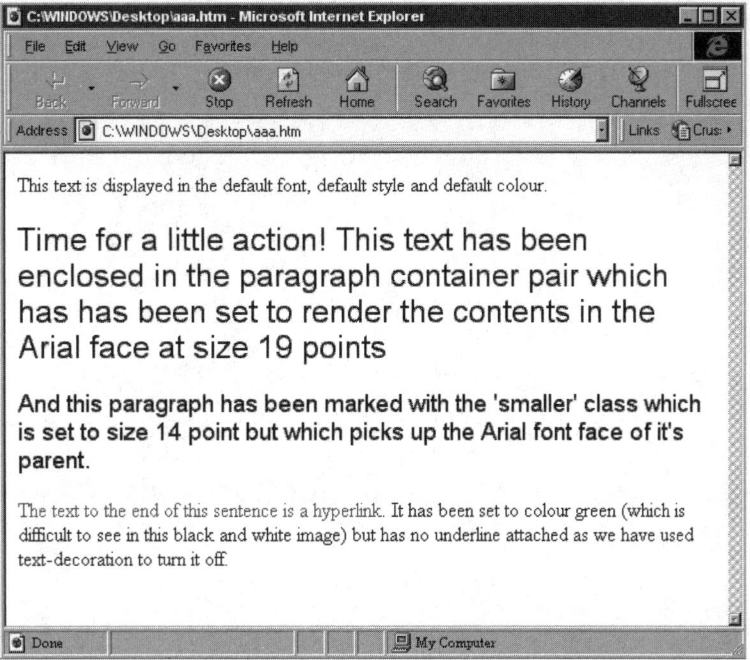

Note the use of the comment tags <!-- and --> to mark off the instructions within the style definition.

If the comments are left out the browser may decide the style commands form part of the displayable document and show them on-screen – which is obviously undesirable.

When utilising style sheets it is always a good idea to include the comments.

Some Useful CSS tags

font-family – allows the fontface to be defined

font-style – defines the text as normal, italic or oblique

font-variant – either normal, or small-caps

font-weight – selects the weight of the font

font-size – defines the physical size of the font

font – allows the above to be defined as a collection

color – defines the colour of an individual element

background-color – sets the background colour of an element

background-image – allows the user to set a background image

background-repeat – defines the way in which the background image is repeated with the browser window

background-attachment – allows the background to be either 'fixed' in the browser or to scroll with the contents

background-position – allows the physical position of the background to be set

background – allows any, or all, of the above to be defined as a collection

word-spacing – allows the space between words to be set

letter-spacing – allows the space between letters to be set

text-decoration – allows decorative effects including underline and bold to be added to text elements

vertical-align – affects the vertical positioning of an element

text-transform – allows text to be capitalized or set to all upper or lowercase

text-align – allows the text in an element to be left, right or centre aligned

text-indent – sets the indentation between the left margin and the first character of a text block

line-height – the vertical distance between text lines

margin-top – sets the top margin of an element

margin-right – sets the right margin of an element

margin-left – sets the left margin of an element

margin – allows any, or all, of the above to be defined as a collection

padding-top – sets the top padding of an element

padding-right – sets the right padding of an element

padding-bottom – sets the bottom padding of an element

padding-left – sets the left padding of an element

padding – allows any, or all, of the above to be defined as a collection

border-top-width – sets the width of an element's top border

border-right-width – sets the width of an element's right border

border-bottom-width – sets the width of an element's bottom border

border-left-width – sets the width of an element's left border

border-width – allows any, or all, of the above to be defined as a collection

border-color – allows the colour of an element border to be defined

border-style – sets the style of the four borders

border-top – sets the style of the top border

border-right – sets the style of the right border

border-bottom – sets the style of the bottom border

border-left – sets the style of the left border

border – allows any, or all, of the above to be defined as a collection

width – allows elements to be scaled in the X direction

height – allows elements to be scaled in the Y direction

float – allows graphic elements to be placed so accompanying text flows around them

For a full and detailed explanation of Cascading style sheets visit:

http://www.w3.org/TR/REC-CSS1-961217.html

Chapter Ten

Dynamic HTML

The introduction of Dynamic HTML in 1997 gave the World Wide Web a whole new look and feel.

In this chapter we'll take a brief look at the basics of this new addition and the potential it offers to the web designer.

Covers

Introduction

In mid 1997 the next phase in the life of the HTML language arrived in the form of Dynamic HTML (or DHTML for short).

By this point in time many developers around the world had outgrown the constraints of the basics of the HTML language and were demanding more functionality, more interactivity and generally more glitzy add-ons than were feasibly possible using the basic instruction set which had evolved from the original idea Tim Berners-Lee had put forward in the 1980s.

Plug-ins and the use of features such as ActiveX and Java applets are all well and good, but they rely on the end user having a machine which can support them and have the patience to download and install any extra pieces of software required to make them work.

Added to this was the massive leap in popularity of the World Wide Web. Five years ago no-one could have anticipated just how popular the Internet would become and demand for access continues to grow in leaps and bounds. This increase in popularity led to many developers creating browsers which were capable of so much more than displaying simple web pages. Users of Microsoft's Internet Explorer browser, for example, may have noticed that if a Word or Excel document is dragged from the desktop and dropped into it the relevant software package is actually opened within the browser window – impressive stuff indeed.

Finally, it is widely accepted that HTML is in a mess. To mid 1997 there was an agreed set of HTML instructions, but many developers have released browsers which have additional functionality built in which gives each variant features which are unavailable in any other.

Something had to be done.

In formulating a new way of looking at the way web browsers should work and in addition adding a whole array of new commands which would extend the functionality of HTML without the need for plug-ins, the W3C launched a project they named Cougar.

Project Cougar aims to alter the way the web is presented by re-defining the standards for HTML from the ground up.

Prior to its inception, the idea was only ever for HTML to display text and images in a certain way, on a single page – with the exception of frames-based pages of course which are slightly different.

Under the new plans the addition of program scripts plays a heavy role, as does more support for simultaneous multiple page control and better facilities for those with disabilities.

What the end result of Project Cougar will be is anybody's guess, a trip to the home pages of the W3C shows even they admit the whole plan is very much under construction and liable to change at regular intervals until they are happy with it. When this will be is open to debate and could take anything from weeks to months.

One thing is for sure, however, the web will never be the same again – even if the current suggestions for command sets and approaches are not altered, the basics are in place to make the World Wide Web a more interesting and interactive place then it has ever been before.

Changes under Project Cougar

In order to make the new HTML standard as flexible as possible there are a number of sweeping changes which are currently being considered.

The most obvious of these is the ability to control and alter every element in a page through scripts.

These scripts, written in languages such as JavaScript and VBScript (see chapter 8) are able to control almost every aspect of the element, from its content to the tags that relate to it.

For example, consider the code fragment:

```
<P>
<B>This is a paragraph of text in bold. <font size=+1>And
this is bold and bigger than the first sentence</FONT></B>
</P>
```

Using procedures and methods suggested within Cougar, it is possible to alter any of the paragraph, bold or font tags by replacing them or changing the parts of the text they affect and it's even possible to alter the text content itself but we'll look at this a little closer in the next chapter.

HANDY TIP

For up-to-the-minute information on Project Cougar visit: http://www.w3.org/MarkUp /Cougar

Absolute and relative positioning has also been introduced which allows the page designer an unprecedented degree of control over where objects are positioned within the browser window.

In HTML standards prior to the HTML 4.0 suggested by Cougar, control over the position of text and pictures was a little rough and ready. True, it is possible to 'cheat' to a degree by using a little lateral thinking, but the designer is severely restricted in a number of different ways – anyone who has tried to position a graphic in an exact position over a background image will sympathise with this view!

Under HTML 4.0 a whole new set of standards have been introduced to deal with this issue. Any element can be placed literally anywhere within the browser and even outside of the displayable area so they can be shuffled on at a later stage.

In addition, support is provided for a pseudo-3D effect which allows the designer to 'layer' text and images.

Dynamic re-drawing of all or part of the page is also supported without the need to re-load the entire page.

The advantage of this, is that changes ranging from modification of a few words in text elements, through to the complete replacement of tables, can be carried out quickly and easily and without the need for long, pointless waiting times as modified pages are downloaded from the server.

These new additions are all well and good but would be totally useless if they were introduced at the expense of previous versions of HTML. After all, if the new commands were incompatible with existing browsers a good many pages coded to the new format would simply 'break' the majority of browsers currently in use rendering the pages unviewable to a huge percentage of those currently surfing the web.

In order to get around this potential problem, the number of new tags which would be added to standard HTML have been kept to a minimum and the new features, in the main, have been included as attributes to the core command set.

The great advantage of this approach is that if an older browser sees a new formatting command it simply ignores it. This is not a perfect solution – nothing ever is – but with a little creative coding it is infinitely possible to produce pages which can be viewed by anyone. This means that users with older browser variants will miss out on any cool new features which have been included but at least the site contents can be seen.

The Document Object Model

In order to implement the new standard the W3C have proposed the introduction of what is known as the Document Object Model.

This object model acts like the skeleton of the new-look standard. As such it provides the bones of any HTML page but is not seen by the page viewer. What the viewer sees is the skin of the page – which in reality is the material created by the actual HTML instructions.

This skeleton covers every aspect of the way HTML interacts with the browser itself, from a control level (how program scripts can trap events such as keypresses or mouseclicks) through to the way stylesheets are applied.

The Document Object Model is a hierarchical structure. Going back to the skeleton analogy, the body object branches from the document object, which in turn branches from the window object in the same way the wrist is connected to the arm which is connected to the shoulder.

Browser Compatibility

Because the definition of Cougar is still not fixed it has been difficult for the brains at Netscape and Microsoft to second guess what the standards board of the W3C will finally agree as the final standard.

Current versions of both browsers have made efforts to implement the latest suggestions but, obviously, neither are perfect.

Netscape is running behind Internet Explorer at the current time by virtue of the fact Netscape launched their Communicator browser well ahead of the Microsoft version. For the first time in the on-going 'browser war' however, both parties have agreed to redefine their projects at such a time as the W3C finally ratify the Cougar proposal.

As it was launched several months later than its counterpart, Internet Explorer adheres much closer to the latest HTML 4.0 proposals and has indeed gone one step further by integrating itself with the Windows 95 and Windows NT operating systems, providing features including the Active Desktop, which allows content to be attached to the OS desktop and the all-new Channel Definition Format which allows server-pushed content to be selected by the viewer and downloaded and viewed at will.

To find out how to make your DHTML operate properly in both Microsoft and Netscape browsers visit: http://www.dhtmlzone.com/articles/dhtml.html

This leaves the designer with a difficult choice - to design for the Microsoft product or that of Netscape. There's no easy way around this situation until the W3C ratify Cougar/HTML 4.0 so it leaves little choice.

If a page relies on dynamic code to achieve its purpose, perhaps it is possible to produce two different versions of the same page, utilising the strengths of Internet Explorer in one, and Netscape in the other. The only way to ensure this can take place is to implement suitable code to check which browser is being used.

DHTML and Internet Explorer 4

Full documentation on DHTML and IE4 can be found at: http://www.microsoft.com/workshop/author/dhtml

Microsoft have gone to great lengths with their version of HTML 4.0... the in-built HTML standard of their Internet Explorer 4 browser.

Broadly speaking this version of the update can be split into three compact sections:

Dynamic content

This heading covers the portion of the implementation which handles the way in which text is displayed within the browser window.

A whole host of attributes have been included to allow a number of ways in which text can be replaced, deleted and inserted.

Using attributes like InnerText and InnerHtml the physical content and even the HTML tags within areas of a page can be changed on the fly according to different situations.

These functions can prove invaluable in situations where, for example, it is desirable to include new levels of interaction.

A good example of this might be a site navigation system where a short paragraph of explanatory text can be displayed onscreen in the form of a mini help system when the user moves the mouse over a particular menu item.

Prior to the new introductions such a facility would only have been possible by using complicated Java applets or script routines. Thankfully DHTML takes all the pain out of the procedure making it much easier and therefore more accessible to the less technically inclined.

The content elements also make it possible to build entire tables of page contents as soon as the page is downloaded to the visitors browsers. The beauty of this facility is that the DHTML code only needs to be written once and can adapt to any changes in the page code a designer may make as updates take place.

With the introduction out of the way, it's time to get down to the serious business of looking at a couple of examples.

The following code makes use of the JavaScript scripting language (see chapter eight for more details). There are many good sources of online information which provide an excellent introduction to the process of scripting and it is recommended that you consult one of these for an in-depth view before plunging into the depths of Dynamic HTML.

Example 1

This simple example demonstrates the basics of using DHTML to change style information within a document.

```
<HTML>
<HEAD>
<TITLE>DHTML Example1</TITLE>
<SCRIPT LANGUAGE="JavaScript">
function modifycode() {
   document.all.Head.style.color = "green";
   document.all.cliktext.innerText = "Tada! See what you can do
with a little imagination?";
}
</SCRIPT>
<BODY>
<CENTER>
<FONT COLOR="red"><H3 ID="Head">Change your
colours whenever you please!</H3>
<P ID="cliktext" ONCLICK="modifycode()">Click me and see
what occurs ....</P>
</CENTER>
</BODY>
</HTML>
```

We'll start by looking at the basic operation of this page, which is carried out by the code within the <BODY> of the document:

```
<BODY>
<CENTER>
<FONT COLOR="red"><H3 ID="Head">Change your
colours whenever you please!</H3>
<P ID="cliktext" ONCLICK="modifycode()">Click me and see
what occurs ....</P>
</CENTER>
</BODY>
```

What this code segment does is to write two text sentences to the screen "Change your colours whenever you please!" and "Click me and see what occurs...". This code in itself is not very exciting, the clever bits come with the introduction of the ID attribute and the ONCLICK command.

In essence, the ID attribute gives a special name to the tag to which it is attached, in this case the H3 tag. We'll come back to the importance of this in a moment and it is important to point out that any number of tags can be referenced using the same ID.

The following line of code assigns another special name, cliktext, to the paragraph tag in addition to the ONCLICK command which transfers control of the webpage to the JavaScript routine called modifycode if, and only if, the user presses the mousebutton over the text "Click me and see what occurs...".

Now take a look at the JavaScript code itself. Each instruction is executed in order from first to last. The first instruction looks through all of the tags (and their associated IDs) until it finds the one specified by the user. In this case HEAD. What happens next is that the COLOR attribute of any and all elements called HEAD are changed to that specified.

In this instance the text is initially set to red, however when the user clicks over the text, thus firing up the JavaScript code, the colour of that text is changed to green. It is important to note that the change will be reflected across anything within the tag which contains a HEAD reference.

Next, the JavaScript turns its attention to the tag referred to by the ID “cliktext”, which is a <P> tag. This time around the command tells the browser to take the text within the tag (by using the innertext attribute) and alter it to something new.

And that’s all there is to it! Take some time to have a good look through this example and understand what is happening. If you have a copy of Internet Explorer installed on your machine type it in and play around with it.

Dynamic Styles

This area of the Microsoft implementation deals with the colours, typefaces, spacing, indentation and even the visibility of the text and images within a page.

Using the navigation example mentioned on the previous page it is possible to extend the interactivity of the menu system, by changing the colour of an item when the mouse is moved over it and increasing its type size slightly to make it obvious to the page viewer which item is about to be selected.

The styles option also provides greatly extended support for typeface provision. As we saw in chapter 2 it is possible to change the fontface used within a page using <FONT FACE="....">, however, the success of this command relies on the page visitor having the necessary fonts installed on their machine. With its 4.0 extensions Microsoft allows fonts to be embedded within the document through the use of a small utility which scans the fonts in a given page and creates a subset of that font which contains only the letters and other symbols which are used within that page.

The benefit of this is that the embedded font can be saved to the server and downloaded along with the page (in much the same way as images are). As a result the previous constraints placed on font use no longer apply.

Extra support has even been added for printing. One of the major complaints of post-4.0 HTML, was that when printing pages there was no control over where pages sent to the printer would begin and end. The result of this lack of control was that hardcopies of web pages could look very untidy and unprofessional.

Thanks to the introduction of new formatting commands it's now possible to force page breaks within HTML documents, making it possible to produce printed content that looks as good on paper as it does electronically.

Example 2

```
<HTML>
<HEAD><TITLE>DHTML Example 2</TITLE>
<SCRIPT LANGUAGE="JavaScript">
function modifytext() {
   document.all.MyHeading.outerHTML = "<H1
ID=MyHeading>Dynamic HTML!</H1>";
   document.all.MyHeading.style.color = "green";
   document.all.MyText.innerText = "You can do the most
amazing things with the least bit of effort.";
   document.all.MyText.align = "center";
  document.body.insertAdjacentHTML("BeforeEnd", "<P
ALIGN=\"center\">Just give it a try!</P>");
}
</SCRIPT>
```

```
<BODY onclick="modifytext()">
<H3 ID=MyHeading>Welcome to Dynamic HTML!</H3>
<P ID=MyText>Click anywhere in this document.</P>
</BODY>
</HTML>
```

As with the last example here we can roughly divide the code into two parts, the raw HTML and the JavaScript code.

Again, the two text sentences contain IDs which will be referenced by the script, the difference here is that in order to trigger the change code the page visitor can click the mouse anywhere in the page, this has been achieved by attaching the ONCLICK command to the BODY tag.

Once the code has been triggered control passes to the JavaScript routine called modifytext().

The first statement in the function modifies the actual HTML code which is rendered to the page, replacing the original <H3> heading code and its associated text with a <H1> heading and different contents. This is followed immediately by a call which changes the colour of the new text to green.

Changing tack slightly, statements three through to five alter the text of the paragraph with the ID MyText through the innerHtml command before centring that text on the page by adding the style attribute CENTER.

This then proves to be the key to the operation of the rather unwieldy looking final statement which does several things all at the same time.

To begin with, the code tells the browser to attach some new code to the BODY tag at the end of all existing HTML, using the "BeforeEnd" attribute. What is attached is a new paragraph tag within associated CENTER attribute set – as the browser interprets this new code as standard HTML it is the equivalent of typing <P ALIGN=CENTER> when creating the page in the first place.

Finally the text string “Just give it a try!” is appended to the code created above.

Dynamic Positioning

The final major area covers the placement of any item within the browser window.

Once again the deficiencies of standard HTML are resolved, and elements can be placed with pixel precision anywhere within the browser window (and in some cases outside of the displayable area).

The opportunities created by this facility are enormous as it’s now possible to move graphics and other elements around the browser window as the viewer sees the page. The dynamic positioning functions even make it possible to create simple games within the browser window like the old arcade favourites Space Invaders and Asteroids – powerful stuff.

Example 3

```
<HTML>
<HEAD><TITLE>DHTML Example 3</TITLE>
<SCRIPT LANGUAGE="JScript">
var id;
function StartGlide()
{
 document.all.moveme.style.pixelLeft =
     document.body.offsetWidth;
  document.all.moveme.style.visibility = "visible";
  id = window.setInterval("Glide()",50);
}
function Glide()
{
  document.all.moveme.style.pixelLeft -= 10;
```

```
    if (document.all.moveme.style.pixelLeft<=0) {
        document.all.moveme.style.pixelLeft=0;
        window.clearInterval(id);
    }
}
</SCRIPT>
<BODY onload="StartGlide()">
<H3>Static content is a thing of the past!</H3>
<P>With dynamic positioning, you can move images
anywhere in the document even
while the user views the document.
<IMG ID="moveme"
STYLE="visibility:hidden;position:absolute;top:0; left:0; z-index:-
1" SRC="banner.gif">
</BODY>
</HTML>
```

As usual, the code proper starts with the BODY tag which contains the onload command. This tells the browser to execute the command contained in the "" as soon as the page and all of its attendant images and other elements have been fully loaded.

That content consists of a short paragraph of descriptive text and an image (banner.gif) which is referenced with the ID "moveme". Notice the STYLE information attached to the IMG which introduces the concept of dynamic positioning. This particular tag tells the browser to start with the graphic displayed invisibly – i.e. it exists on the page but is not in view in its initial state. Further, the position of the image is specified at the absolute coordinates 0,0, or top left. Using dynamic positioning, elements can be given absolute positions which are specified in relation to the top left corner of the browser display area or relative to the position they would normally occupy on the page.

Once this image and the text have been loaded and displayed the onload event fires and control passes to the JavaScript function StartGlide() which will begin the movement of the image proper.

What StartGlide() does is to determine how many pixels wide the browser display area is (gleaned through document.body.offsetwidth) then sets the X coordinate of the image (or left as it's called) to that value. It follows this off by making the image visible to the page viewer and then sets up a special routine through window.setInterval which in turn fires off the function called Glide(). What's clever about window.setInterval is that it calls a given function every x miliseconds, in this case the function call is to Glide() and the call is carried out every 50 milliseconds. Making this number larger or smaller will have the effect of speeding up, or slowing down, the speed at which the image 'moves' across the browser.

The Glide function itself starts by subtracting 10 from the value of the image's current x coordinate, next up a check is made is see if that value is less than or equal to zero – if this happens of course it indicates that the image has reached the left hand side of the browser display area. If this is the case the value of the x coordinate is set to zero (we don't want it to be less than that, otherwise the image would start to disappear off the left hand edge) and finally the setInterval is cancelled to prevent further pointless movements of the image being made.

And there you have it, dynamic movement of elements within the browser window as visitors read the text. Clever stuff indeed!

The three examples given so far demonstrate the three fundamental concepts of what can be achieved with dynamic HTML. The final example draws many of these elements together in creating a mini website which displays a number of images from a web gallery.

The main screen, pictured below, shows the initial state of the program, with a small menu to the left of the screen and a selection of images on the right.

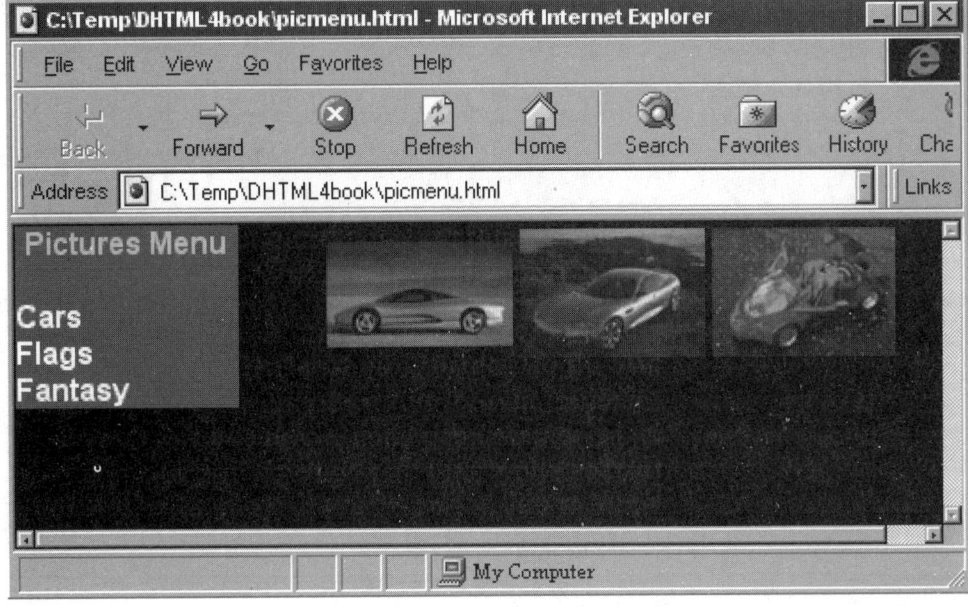

Each of the images displayed is a thumbnail impression of a much larger picture which sits on the server. Thumbnails are often used to show small representations of the full image as they are much quicker to load and give the page visitor an opportunity to see what it is they have the option of viewing without the necessity of downloading huge files they may not want.

The idea behind this program is to dynamically change the thumbnails, and the links to their parent images, depending on which menu option from the left is selected.

The code to carry this out is given below followed by a full explanation.

```
<html>
<head>
<script language="javascript">
function changepage(change){
	//Dynamically change the thumbnail and master image
HREF
	for (loop=0; loop<3;loop++){
		document.images(loop).src = change+"/
"+(loop+1)+"icon.jpg";
		document.links(loop).href = change+"/
"+(loop+1)+".jpg";
	}

}
function hilite(){
	window.event.srcElement.style.color="darkgreen";
	window.event.srcElement.style.cursor="hand";
}

function lolite(){
	window.event.srcElement.style.color="white";
}
</script>
</head>
```

...contd

```
<body bgcolor="black" text="white">
<font face="arial, helvetica">
<div id="menu" style="position: absolute; top:0; left:0;
width=120; height=120;background-color='green';">
<center><b><font color="lightgreen">Pictures Menu</
font></b></center><p>
<div id="cars" onmousedown="changepage('cars')"
onmouseover="hilite()" onmouseout="lolite()">
<b>Cars</b>
</div>

<div id="flags" onmousedown="changepage('flags')"
onmouseover="hilite()" onmouseout="lolite()">
<b>Flags</b>
</div>

<div id="fantasy" onmousedown="changepage('fantasy')"
onmouseover="hilite()" onmouseout="lolite()">
<b>Fantasy</b>
</div>
</div>
<div id="displayarea" style="position:absolute; top:0; left:121;
width=400;background-color='black'">
<center>
<table width="50%" border=0>
<tr>
<td>
<div id="pic1">
<a href="cars/1.jpg"><img src="cars/1icon.jpg"
border=0></a>
```

```
</div>
</td>
<td>
<div id="pic2">
<a href="cars/2.jpg"><img src="cars/2icon.jpg"
border=0></a>
</div>
</td>
<td>
<div id="pic3">
<a href="cars/3.jpg"><img src="cars/3icon.jpg"
border=0></a>
</div>
</td>
</tr>
</table>
</center>
</div>
</font>
</body>
</html>
```

Whilst this is a very long example, it's interesting to dissect it and see just what is going on.

As with all of our examples so far, the action begins with the execution of the HTML formatting commands within the <BODY> of the document.

In this case, the overall background colour and text colours are set followed by the font face for the document.

The first <DIV>, which carries the ID "menu" defines an onscreen area which is anchored to the top left corner of the browser display area, is 120 pixels wide and 120 high with a background colour set to green.

The code which follows displays a title for the menu followed by three options titled cars, flags and fantasy. Each option is contained by its own <DIV> and each contains code which will handle three different events which cater for situations where a visitor moves the mouse over a particular menu item (onmouseover), moves it away from an item (onmouseout) or chooses an option by pressing the left mouse button (onmousedown).

In the event of a mouseover, control is passed to the JavaScript function hilite() which discovers which page element has been "activated" using window.event.srcElement and changes its colour to dark green. In addition this routine changes the mouse pointer to a hand to show the visitor that what lies beneath is a hyperlink.

When the mouse is moved off an item lolite() is called which simply resets the colour of the active element to white.

Most importantly, if the user moves the mouse over a menu item and selects that item by clicking on it, control is passed to the function called changepage which takes a single parameter called change.

In the following lines a loop is started which counts from zero to two (the first element of any type in a collection or page is always item zero).

The code within the loop starts by modifying the position from which the browser obtains its images, using the value held in change to provide it with the relevant webserver subdirectory.

Imagine it this way. Our gallery page contains three sections – cars, flags and fantasy pictures. Each set of pictures is held in their own subdirectory on the server.

In standard HTML if we wanted to allow visitors to access our picture sets it would be necessary to write three similar HTML files each of which pointed directly to the contents of a particular subdirectory.

The only difference between the files would be the links and the thumbnails which are displayed onscreen so each HTML tag would look something like this:

```
<A HREF="cars/1.jpg"><IMG SRC="cars/1icon.jpg"></a>
```

What the DHTML code does is to change the “cars” portion of the <A HREF..> and <IMG ...> tags directly to which ever option has been selected.

As soon as the browser detects the change it updates its contents and replaces the thumbnail images with the new ones and also amends the pictures to which the thumbnails point.

This example shows how, with a little thought, dynamic HTML can be used to save time and effort whilst still retaining full functionality. It can also save webspace as the HTML file only needs to be written once instead of three times, reducing the number of required files.

DHTML and Netscape 4

For their first implementation of Dynamic HTML, Netscape have taken a very different approach to that of Microsoft.

The code built into their Communicator browser provides some of the same functionality as the Internet Explorer variant but falls short of their rivals implementation.

Unfortunately, the Communicator view of Dynamic HTML does not allow access to page contents once that page is loaded. Some items, such as frames, plug-ins, links, images, and style sheets, are still fully accessible but beyond that things come to a rather sudden halt.

One area in which Communicator does score a point over Explorer, however, is in its support for a technique called layering.

The layering concept works in much the same way as traditional cartooning techniques, in which the overall image is built up using a number of elements painted onto clear acetate sheets which are placed one on top of another.

Such an approach allows portions of the whole image to be altered and adapted without the necessity of changing the entire construction.

Using such layers electronically within Communicator, in conjunction with a suitable scripting language means a variety of effects can be achieved.

For example, the interactive navigation system we discussed earlier in this chapter could be coded for Navigator, but some elements, such as the explanatory text for the menu items, would be written to different layers and the layers made visible or invisible to suit a particular situation.

Although it may seem at this very basic introductory level that Netscape is a long way behind its competitor, Communicator's implementation of DHTML is very powerful and should not be underestimated by any means.

The following examples give a little insight into the inner workings of the <LAYER> tag.

Example 1

The following code sets up three layers onscreen each of which contains its own content.

Note that the layer definitions can be placed anywhere within the HTML document. When Communicator discovers a layer definition it is quite happy to break away from the normal linear rendering mode for the page and set about the dynamic positioning of the new element.

```
<HTML>
<HEAD>
<TITLE>Netscape Layer Test</TITLE>
</HEAD>

<BODY>

<!-- default units for TOP, LEFT, and WIDTH is pixels -->
<LAYER ID="layer1" TOP=20pt LEFT=5pt
BGCOLOR="#CC00EE" WIDTH=250 HEIGHT=300>
 <H1>This is Layer 1</H1>
  <IMG SRC="3.jpg" align=right>
</LAYER>

<LAYER ID="layer2" TOP=60 LEFT=150 BGCOLOR=teal
WIDTH=200>
 <P>Layer 2 goes here</P>
</LAYER>
```

```
<LAYER ID="layer3" TOP=270 LEFT=125
BGCOLOR="#6666FF">
 <H1>Layer 3</H1>
 <P>Using LAYERS you can place content anywhere on the
page.</P>
</LAYER>
</BODY>
</HTML>
```

Notice how each layer is given its own ID attribute and is given its absolute position within the browser display area through the use of the TOP and LEFT attributes.

The end result of the code above is given below:

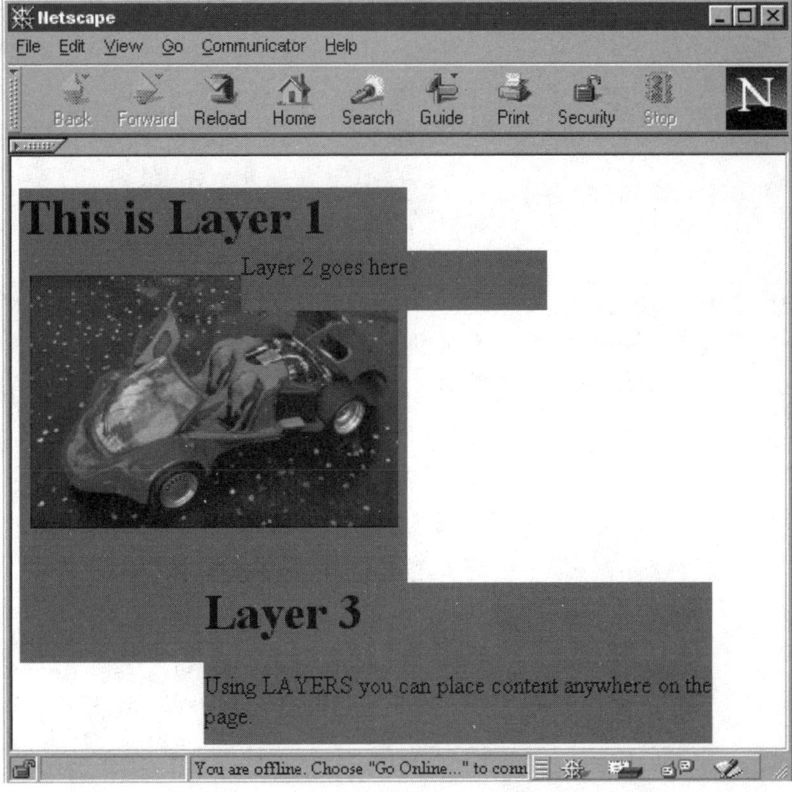

It is also possible to attach stylesheets directly to Netscape's layers, giving a degree of extra control to the way pages can be constructed.

Example 2

```
<HTML>
<HEAD>
<STYLE TYPE="text/css">
<!--
 all.style4 {
 color:magenta;
 border-width:20px; border-color:cyan;
 border-style:ridge;
 padding:5%;
}
-->
</STYLE>
</HEAD>
<BODY BGCOLOR=white>
<LAYER ID=layer4 TOP=30 LEFT=100 BGCOLOR=yellow
   CLASS=style4>
<center>
 <H1>HELLO!</H1>
 <P>Layers can be stylish and colourful too.</P>
</center>
</LAYER>
</BODY>
</HTML>
```

Notice here how all of the formatting information has been included within the stylesheet definition, which is attached to the layer definition through the use of the CLASS attribute.

There are two major advantages to adopting this approach to coding for layers – although the practice could be equally adopted for any HTML code which includes stylesheets.

The most obvious is that the styles only ever need to be defined once and can be used liberally throughout a particular page without the need for laborious repetition. Secondly, the stylesheet information helps to take the confusion out of what could be long and complicated definition statements.

The results of the code for this example are shown below:

Further Reading

As you may have gathered by this point Dynamic HTML is a very involved subject which can take some real study to use effectively.

Luckily there are plenty of helpful people on the web who provide resources which are free to site visitors. Browse through some of these excellent offerings for loads of help and tips suitable for all levels of DHTML experience.

http://www.microsoft.com/workshop/author/dhtml/
DHTML according to Microsoft

http://www.microsoft.com/sitebuilder/
In-depth information for developers

http://developer.netscape.com/one/dynhtml/index.html
Netscape introduces layers here

http://www.projectcool.com/developer/
Project Cool's guide to DHTML

http://www.stars.com
The web developers virtual library

http://www.htmlguru.com
A truly beautiful site which informs and entertains

http://www.dhtmlzone.com/index.html
Macromedia's Dynamic HTML zone, also includes extensive information on integrating DHTML and their excellent Shockwave product

Chapter Eleven

CGI

There are situations where it is necessary to collect data from web page visitors. Generally speaking, basic HTML isn't up to the task.

In order to allow the designer to access this information it is necessary to resort to server side solutions controlled by CGI.

Covers

What is CGI?

There are times when standard HTML is just not enough.

When the standards for the language and the browsers which would interpret it were defined, it was decided to make the whole thing as safe as possible – and safe meant that it was impossible to do anything that affects a viewer's machine 'outside' of the browser.

In the main this is a great idea, as it means that malicious 'hackers' can't write code which will damage a visitor's computer.

For all of its advantages however, there are times when it's desirable to be able to write files on a server, deal with data from fill-in forms (see chapter six for more) or create HTML pages 'on the fly'.

CGI (Common Gateway Interface) allows all of the above to take place, providing a standard channel between the web page and special CGI scripts which sit on the web server.

The scripts are sets of commands which can be called from the browser but they are in no way interactive and it is not possible to get a script to ask the user directly for input, the input must be passed from the browser in some way – from a form for example.

Data coming as output from a script can be in any form; as HTML, standard text, even graphic files.

It is important to note from the outset that CGI is very complex and a good knowledge of programming languages and techniques is necessary.

The more common CGI scripts, which perform a variety of tasks including outputting the current time, keeping count of the number of visitors to a page or allowing guestbooks to be maintained, can be downloaded as pre-written modules and placed straight into your own code.

CGI Languages

There are many programming languages available today which are built for a variety of tasks.

Some, like Fortran, are geared towards solving complex mathematical problems, others like COBOL, for database handling.

For the purposes of the Web and CGI many of these better known languages are totally unsuitable.

There are two major problems in finding a good CGI language.

The first is that scripts need to run quickly – very quickly in fact. If they fail to execute within a short space of time the server will assume the script has failed in some way and return an error.

Perhaps more importantly, because of the security implications of running scripts, many webmasters will want to thoroughly vet any programs you may wish to include in your site.

As a result of this any compiled languages (C, C++, even BASIC) are usually ruled out and only interpreted languages (those which are executed in real-time a line at a time) are allowed – unless you happen to own your own web server of course.

For this reason the number of CGI languages available for general use is restricted and perhaps the most popular of this is a compact package called PERL.

PERL (Practical Extraction and Report Language) was conceived by American computer expert Larry Wall many years ago.

It arose when Wall needed a way to gain quick access to UNIX-based web machines.

As a result the PERL language was born. Given that it was written to interface with UNIX computers PERL is eminently qualified to be both fast and efficient.

The downside to this is that like the vast majority of UNIX-related programming languages, it is far from easy to understand for the beginner and even experienced programmers can experience difficulties with what is regarded in the Net of today as rather an old language.

For the latest information and downloads relating to Perl visit http://www.perl.com

For all of the pros and cons of its design, PERL continues to be the language of choice for the bulk of web programmers and there are many (literally hundreds) of pre-written 'plug-in' library files which help to take the pain out of creating your own code.

Including calls to PERL scripts is as simple as inserting the path to the script into your code.

The path describes the physical location of the script to be executed on the web server – this is usually a special folder or directory called cgi-bin.

In the case of a fictitious visitor counter program which displays a graphic on the page and automatically updates the number of visitors as they arrive the call might be:

```
<img src="/cgi-bin/count">
```

What this call does is to look in the cgi-bin directory for a program called count. The program will return an image which is a graphical representation of the number of visitors to the page which in turn is output through the <IMG SRC...> tag.

If the program were missing, failed to execute properly, or a fault developed on the server, the browser would simply display a symbol to indicate the 'graphic' in question was broken.

For more information on PERL visit:

http://www.perl.com

Server-Side Includes

A recurring question from HTML programmers concerns the inclusion of common portions of code and other information.

Say we have a website design which has the same information at the top of each page. This information, for the sake of argument, displays copyright information and a graphic image which acts as an advertisement for the site owner's other project.

Using standard HTML it would be necessary to include this code in every HTML file on the site – a rather inelegant solution and one which could prove cumbersome if changes are required.

Not all web space providers will allow you to use SSIs. Check carefully before using them.

To circumvent this situation we can use a form of CGI called *Server-Side Includes.*

Rather than using a fully-fledged CGI script it is possible to use a single command which, when executed, tells the server to take a particular image, text file or code fragment and add it into the page being called before it leaves the server and travels to the visitor's browser.

The format of this command is similar to the standard HTML comment tag with a couple of essential differences. Take this example:

```
<!--#include file="myfile.txt" -->
```

Note the inclusion of the #include command directly after the double dashes of the comment tag. This tells the server that what follows is a command and not just a comment. The second part of the command specifies the file to be included within the HTML file and may include the path to the target file relative to the current document.

In this example the contents of myfile.txt would be inserted directly into the HTML file before it is sent to the viewer. Of course, the file could easily be another HTML file as in our next example.

The advantage of using such a technique is obvious, as the common code need only be written once and is then automatically inserted into any page which holds the relevant <!--#include .. --> command.

In addition to file, #include can also take the attribute virtual. For example:

```
<!--#include virtual="/crussell/website/adbanner.html" -->
```

The virtual attribute works differently to file in that it specifies the virtual path to the document starting from the root directory of the server.

Other server-side include commands are:

Echo – allows system variables to be output

FSIZE – prints the size of a specified file (in bytes)

FLASTMOD – gives the 'last modified' date of a file

EXEC – allows a CGI script to be executed

Care should be taken not to overdo the number of Server-Side Includes (SSIs) in a page as each call takes up processor time, increasing the amount of time it takes to deliver the page to the user and, potentially, upsetting other designers who use the same server as you, as access to their pages will be slowed because your creation is taking up so much server time.

For more information on SSI and CGI try these links:

http://hoohoo.ncsa.uiuc.edu/cgi/

http://agora.leeds.ac.uk/nik/Cgi/start.html

http://www.stars.com

Chapter Twelve

Publishing Your Site

So far we've looked at how to use HTML to produce web pages which are suitable for any occasion.

The final stage of the operation is still to come. Once you have designed and built your web pages, you will need to 'publish' them to the web, so other people can see them.

Covers

Uploading Files to the Web

Don't mix case in filenames – try to use all upper or lowercase text in file names. Using mixed case can cause problems with some servers.

The creation of HTML-based pages forms most of the battle of producing web sites, but the greatest site in the world is worthless if no-one can see it.

In order for your site to join the hundreds of thousands of others vying of the attention of Internet users, it is necessary to take every HTML document, graphic, sound file and possibly even Java applet and place them somewhere where anyone can access them.

There are several steps involved in the process which we'll discuss over the next few pages, including finding somewhere to place your masterpiece, and the software required to transfer it from your home/business PC to its permanent site.

Although this part of the process may sound like the easy bit, great care should be taken in 'uploading' your web site.

There's nothing more disappointing than receiving your first e-mails from site visitors only to find the streams of praise you were expecting have been replaced by complaints that something doesn't work properly.

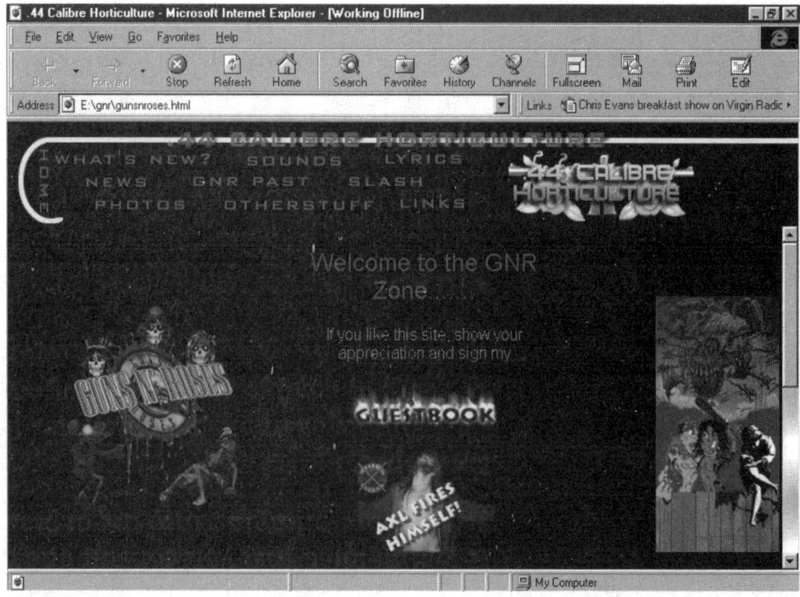

Web Space

Even before the process of uploading your page content begins it is necessary to discover whether or not you have somewhere to place it.

These days many Internet Service Providers (ISPs) include an amount of space as part of the package you buy when you take up an account with them.

The amount of space can vary widely from one megabyte upwards. One UK-based service provider even gives away unlimited space to its subscribers.

It's worthwhile checking with your provider just how much space you have to play with as too big a site will overflow your allocation and you may have to lose some sections of your work in order to make it fit.

If your Internet account doesn't include free web space or the amount you have isn't enough, it's always possible to rent more from one of the many providers which offer such services around the world. It's also worth remembering that because of the nature of the Net your site doesn't have to be hosted in your home country – location loses its importance on the Internet.

For those who don't want to pay for websites there's a cheaper alternative in the form of a number of providers who give webspace away free of charge. For free space try:

http://www.angelfire.com

http://www.geocities.com

Of course, with any space you choose to take up there is an Internet address attached. Some can be simple to remember, for example http://www.yourhost.com/crussell and some can be a little more complex; http://www.ahost.co.uk/pub/users/~crussell. However, for those with a little cash to spare, or for businesses, there is always the option of registering your own web address – see the next topic, Virtual Servers.

Virtual Servers

Once you've registered a domain name and are using it, you can change your service provider without changing your web address that you've promoted.

A number of organisations exist through which it is possible to buy your own 'custom' web address (or domain name) and rent space to host your site at that address. This is particularly useful if your site is a commercial one and you want to create an impression that you've invested in your own dedicated server.

The provider of a virtual server can tweak the setup of just one of their servers to host websites for several companies, making it look like each has its own server, e.g.

http://www.mycompany.com

This is all an illusion – you don't really have your own server, but it's a lot cheaper than having your own dedicated machine connected to the Net 24-hours a day, everyday.

An example of a company providing virtual servers to host your website and registration of domain names is Virtual Internet, found at http://www.vi.net

You can also register your domain name directly with the relevant authorities: for example, via Nominet (http://www.nic.uk) for .co.uk domains or via InterNIC in the USA (http://www.internic.net) for international .com domains.

File Transfer Protocol

Choose your own shareware Windows 95 FTP client from: http:// tucows.cableinet.net/ ftp95.html

With the issue of webspace sorted out the process of uploading your content to your site can begin.

In order to do this we must use the File Transfer Protocol or FTP.

FTP is a special protocol used on the Internet for physically transferring information, data and images between computers. Today it is possible to download files through your web browser but this can be a slow process and not as efficient or effective as using FTP.

The way in which the FTP protocol actually works is unimportant, it is enough to know that we must FTP to get files to the server on which they are to 'live'.

As with the HTTP protocol which requires a special client, or browser, to access, FTP also has a huge number of client programs which take all the pain out of transferring files.

Using these programs is simple and straightforward but care must be taken to make sure you have entered the correct username and password required to give you access to your space.

FTPing Your Site – An Example

With your client installed it's finally time to upload your web content.

The following example uses the CuteFTP client for the PC but most FTP programs operate in a similar way.

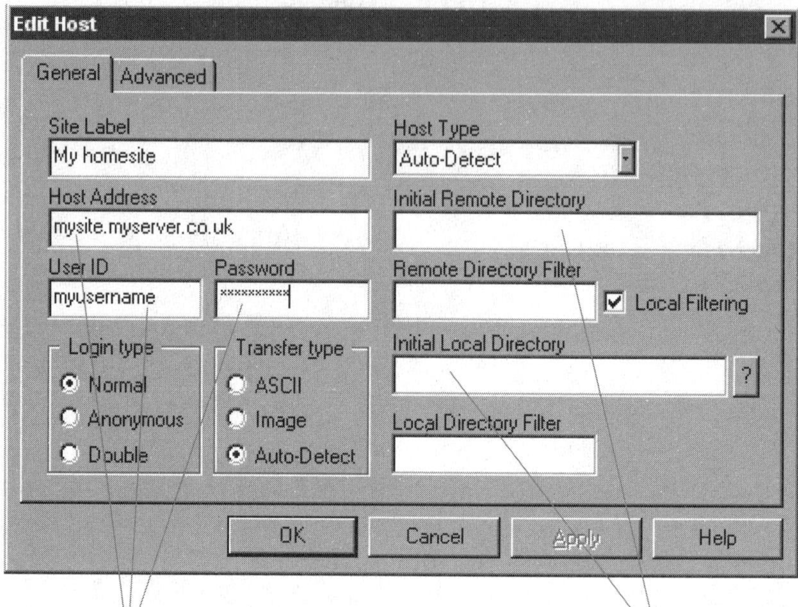

These entry boxes allow the server and password details to be set up.

CuteFTP allows the user to define which directories on the server and the local PC should be used as the default.

The screen above shows how CuteFTP allows the user to set up the details of the server to which the FTP operation will be carried out. The most important details are those which give the physical address of the server, the username and password.

Without this it will be impossible to log on to the server before file transfer can take place.

...contd

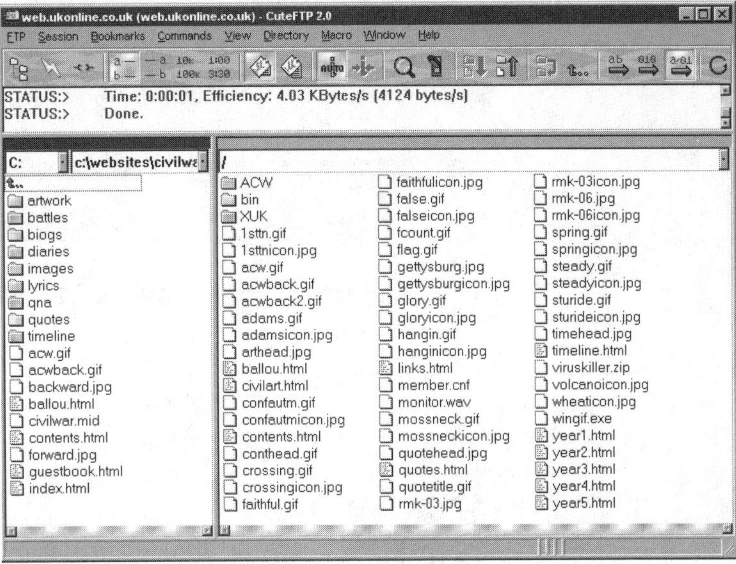

In this image we see the FTP client has logged onto the server. The list of files on the lefthand side of the screen represents the files on the local PC. Those on the righthand side are the files that are currently placed on the server.

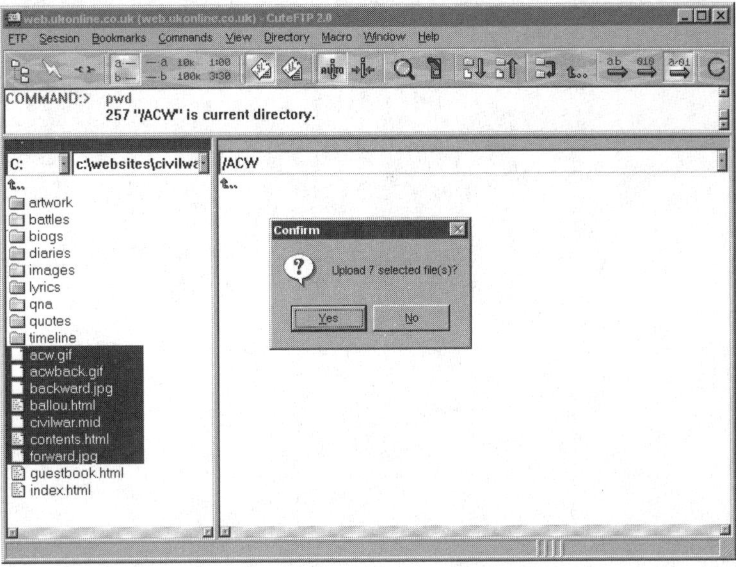

The image overleaf shows seven files have been highlighted and dragged from the left side of the screen to the right – indicating we wish to upload that set of files.

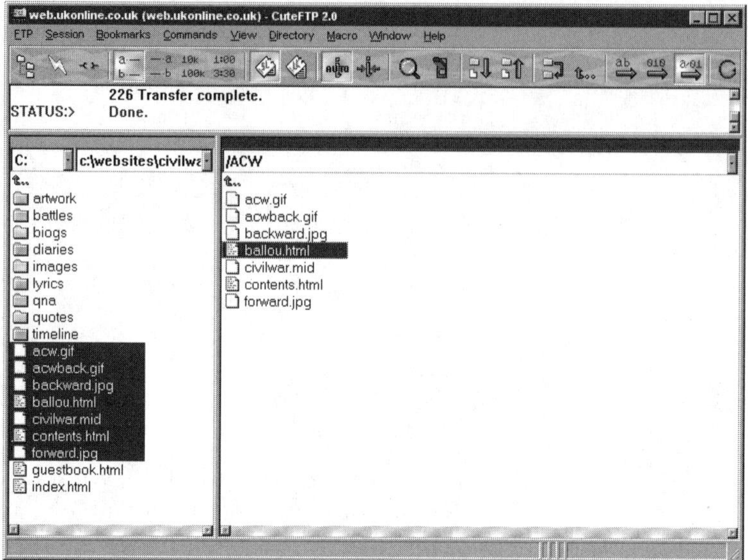

And the result is... success! The files have been successfully transferred across. Now, when visitors enter the site address, they'll see the latest web-creation efforts in place.

Site uploading can take quite some time, depending on how many files are being transferred and how big they are.

To view your uploaded site, all you have to do is type the URL into your browser, for example:

http://www.domain.co.uk/mysite

Chapter Thirteen

HTML With Style

Anyone can learn to write HTML but writing quality code takes a little something extra.

This chapter presents some hints and tips which make life easier for you and for the people who view your site.

Covers

Writing 'good' HTML

By now you should have a fairly good grasp of the basics of the HTML language and how to use it effectively to create web pages. One topic we haven't touched on yet is that of style.

Style is a very subjective matter and open to many differing views but there are some simple rules which can be adopted which will make HTML code easier to read and pages easier to navigate and download.

Thumbing it...

As we've seen, images can be used to great effect to add life to a page. There are many pages on the web today which use lots of images – most notably those pages on sites which act as 'galleries'. It's easy to simply place your images straight into the page and think no more about it.

To the visitor, however, this approach can be intensely annoying, especially if the page in question contains many images and each one is 640 by 480 pixels in size. The time taken to download such a collection of images can be in the region of several minutes and the visitor is quite likely to give up on your efforts and surf off elsewhere without stopping for a proper look.

For an easy way to create thumbnail images download the ThumbsPlus shareware package from: http://www.cerious.com

A far easier way of displaying collections of images without the huge wait is to use thumbnails. To put it simply, thumbnails are small versions of the full-sized image, created within a graphics package by making a copy of the original and using relevant resize options to reduce it down. Usually a horizontal width of between 100 and 150 pixels is sufficient to give the viewer a taster of the full sized picture without the long wait.

In order to give the visitor the opportunity to view the larger image the thumbnail can be made a hyperlink to its bigger brother. For example:

```
<A HREF="bigpic.jpg"><IMG SRC="thumbnail.jpg"
border=0></a>
```

Here, the thumbnail is contained in an anchor container which links to the picture called bigpic.jpg. Notice the use of the attribute BORDER=0. Normally when an image is used as a hyperlink the browser will surround the image with a rather garish looking border which marks it as a link (rather like the underlines used on text). Using BORDER=0 turns the border off displaying the image in its natural form.

Keeping it neat

It's easy in the heat of the creative moment to bash out pages and pages of highly entertaining code and then upload it to your website to the general applause and adulation of your visitors. But without a little thought as to the layout of the HTML file, updating the page at a later date can be a nightmare.

Think carefully and adopt a consistent style throughout your code development. Taking a few moments out to think about the layout can save hours of work later on.

Throughout this book the HTML tags have been written in capitals. It is not essential to do this and any combination of upper and lower case characters can be used but using capitals helps to differentiate the tags from the text which will appear in the browser window. It's a small thing but in the long run it can be very helpful when updating or re-writing parts of your site.

Commenting your code

This handy hint goes hand in glove with the tip above and concerns good housekeeping in the way you create your pages.

Back in chapter 2 in our discussion of the basic commands of HTML the comment container pair (<!-- and -->) were introduced. If you look back you'll find that whatever text is contained within the comment containers it does not actually appear on the page, it's only there to allow the designer to include notes to him or herself.

It's this note making ability that holds the attraction. Say you've written a page with a highly complicated frameset and each page within the frameset contains multiple tables.

Writing it in the first instance is the easy part but what happens three months later when it comes to updating the pages with new information?

Chances are you may have forgotten how the designs worked and it will take a fair amount of time to sit and work out exactly what each code portion did.

Judicious use of comments can help prevent this – feel free to use as many as you feel necessary, after all no-one will see them but you.

Special Effects

There are so many things which are possible using HTML that it's difficult to know how to shoehorn them all into one page – DON'T!

Get the book, Web Page Design in easy steps, in this same series.

With special effects, less is definitely more and one carefully placed animated graphic can have a greater effect on visitors than a dozen which have been spotted at random across the page.

Just because you can include video clips, sound files, flashing pictures and more doesn't mean you should. Take time to think carefully about placement and regularity of your 'eyecandy'.

On similar lines take care when using background images and colours. The background should complement any foreground and text colours you use and the text should be clear and easy to read. Discovering the meaning of life and creating a webpage to share it with the world is a pointless exercise if no-one reads what you've found.

Font faces should also be used with care. Restrict the number of faces on a page to a couple at most.

Overuse of fonts can be as confusing and off-putting as over-enthusiastic backgrounds.

Link Checking

We've mentioned this in an earlier chapter, but it's worth repeating if only to help you lose face when your page goes 'live' on the web. Check all links thoroughly.

Link check the easy way with the shareware version of the excellent Linkbot package from: http://tetranetsoftware.com

It doesn't matter if the links are internal (point to other pages within your site) or external (other people's sites) it only takes a little time to make sure they've all been correctly entered in your code.

Bear in mind it's frustrating for a visitor to click on a link that doesn't take them anywhere.

Building in flexibility

Even before sitting down to start coding take a little time to think about your target audience.

If you're setting out to make your site available to the widest possible audience it's necessary to stick to the most standard of HTML commands so that code will be correctly interpreted by the maximum number of browsers.

If, on the other hand, you decide to use the special effects of Internet Explorer 4 with its wide support for Dynamic HTML feel free to do but it may be a good idea to make the first page of your website a warning screen which advises visitors of the software they'll need to get the best from it.

Think also about providing support for people with differing screen sizes. Just because your monitor supports a resolution of 800 x 600 pixels it doesn't mean everyone's will.

If your site is designed for a particular screen size tell people. If you wish to make it more accessible make sure everything will fit happily into an area no wider than 640 pixels – that way everyone will be happy.

Learning from others

The best way to learn new tricks and techniques is to take a look at what others have done.

Nearly all browsers contain an option which allows the visitor to view the source code of the page they are viewing.

Feel free to take a look at what others have done and how they achieved some of their special effects. You'll be amazed at what you can pick up.

Keeping up-to-date with developments

The Web is a constantly changing place. Every day, it seems, there are new coding standards, plug-ins and development technologies being introduced.

The truly enthusiastic Web fan can keep up to date with all the latest news and information by checking out information sites regularly.

The best sites on which to start are those run by software manufacturers, news sites and standards organisations.

Why not try:

http://www.microsoft.com – home to Internet Explorer

http://www.netscape.com - home site of Netscape Navigator

http://www.zdnet.com - an excellent news site updated daily

There are of course plenty more, but these three should be enough to get you going.

Stylish Sites

There are many tens of thousands of sites out on the web ranging from simple homepages to sprawling sites dedicated to some of the world's biggest companies.

As you would expect not all of them are sparkling examples of what can be achieved with HTML and a little creative spark.

However every now and again comes a site which shows off the web at its best. Take a visit to the sites below and see what can be achieved with a little imagination and style.

http://www.mtv.com – a thoroughly engaging frames-based site to promote the activities of this popular satellite music station

http://www.disney.com – a sample of what can be achieved with high-quality graphics

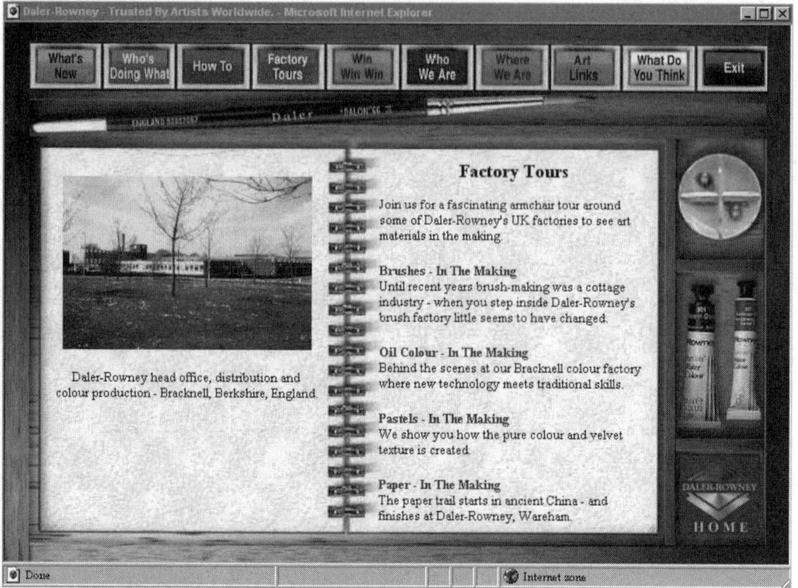

http://www.daler-rowney.com – a unique site designed to look like an artist's paintbox

http://www.schweppes.com – a well executed site which ably demonstrates how to use the Macromedia Shockwave plug-in

http://www.htmlguru.com – a great introduction to the world of dynamic HTML and a beautiful design

http://www.whatsnew.com/id/ – Internet directory UK – check this site regularly for the newest web sites in the UK

...contd

http://www.christmas.uk.com – an excellent example of how HTML and high quality graphics combine to produce a compelling web experience

http://www.sony.com – the Japanese electronics experts have produced a site which embodies a simple design with strong content

http://www.brainstormers.com – dark, industrial-style graphics and strong use of animated images are combined in this homesite for a UK-based web design house

Some Final Thoughts...

In this chapter we've looked at some pointers to producing "good" HTML and had a browse through some of the better designed sites on the web and by now you'll be itching to fire up an HTML editor and start your own fantastic creations.

Before you do so just take a minute to think about what you're doing and ask: "Do I really have a clear idea of what it is I'm trying to achieve and how am I going to set about it?".

It might sound like a rather dull and uninteresting thing to consider when faced with the alternative of bashing out some code and putting your name all over the world of electronic publishing but it's fair to say that the majority of home pages on the net today are classic examples of poor pre-planning.

It needn't be a long task either, jot down a few notes on how you want your site to look, if you're going to implement a navigational system think carefully about how it will work – are you going to code all of the options onto every page you write or use frames to hold your nav bar and main pages – think carefully about the use of images and sound too and make sure they're not too big and will fit into the style of your page. The more planning you do at this stage in the site design the less work you'll have to do to produce a site which you're happy with and the rest of the world will flock to see.

And finally, if you want to see how **NOT** to do it properly, fire up your browser and nip over to:

http://www.webpagesthatsuck.com

Chapter Fourteen

Publicising Your Site

Many people think that once the act of physically building a website has been completed the Internet 'battle' is over.

This assumption is far from the truth as it's now necessary to tell the surfing public what you have to offer and where it is. Time then for a short discussion on electronic publicity.

Covers

Why Publicise?

Imagine for a moment that you've built the world's greatest website. Its graphics are better than anything yet produced and its content is in-depth, comprehensive and extremely well written.

Following all of the correct procedures the completed HTML files and accompanying images and sounds have been uploaded to a server and checked to make sure everything is in order. All that remains is to sit back and wait for the visitors to come flooding in.

The problem is, that in spite of all the hard work ploughed into this masterpiece no-one visits because they don't even know it exists.

Over time a small number of visitors may pop in because they stumble over your work purely by chance and it's entirely possible they may tell their friends and colleagues who in turn will visit. In time you may get dozens of hits to your site. But that's not very impressive is it?

Everyone wants to have a successful and popular site which is known across the web and the only way to ensure your message gets across is to publicise it.

There are several ways to accomplish this, some of which are totally free, others (as ever) involve a degree of cost.

It is possible to successfully advertise your skills and content without ever opening your wallet, but you can be sure that a little paid-for advertising will work wonders – particularly if you run a business site.

Search Engines

Search engines are among the most popular sites on the entire Internet and for good reason.

A search engine is the Net equivalent of the yellow pages. It is a huge database of web sites and other resources which can be searched by visitors in order to obtain a list of websites pertinent to a particular query.

For example, entering the words 'computer games' into a facility such as Yahoo (http://www.yahoo.com) will return a huge list of sites which contain the words "computer" and "games", giving the visitor plenty of starting points for information in that particular area.

Obviously, entering the details for your own site into such a facility is a good idea as it logs your information with the engine, opening up the site information, its URL and a brief description of what it's all about to a potential audience of millions of people straight away.

There are a growing number of search engines across the Net, all of which are used heavily by surfers. Entering the same set of details about your site into each one can be a very time-consuming and tedious task.

It's a good job then that some enterprising souls provide websites which allow you to enter the details once and then send them off to numerous places around the web.

Many such sites will send the information to perhaps 20 or 30 such search engines and want you to part with hard cash before carrying on to several hundred more, but the sites covered within the initial free part of the deal should provide a solid start.

The information requested is usually quite straightforward, consisting of your name and e-mail address, the title of the site, a short description of what it's all about and perhaps even a list of keywords which best describe what your site does.

In order to save on-line time and to prevent spending time trying to make up this information straight off the top of your head, it's often best to sit down before registering and plan what you want to say. This will also prevent you from making mistakes and having to go through the whole registration process again.

Making the search engines take notice

In order to get the best from the search engines it is best to tell it how you want your site to be searched and subsequently indexed.

Ordinarily, the bulk of search engines will visit your site and index every word they find before creating a short description from the first few text sentences on the page.

In some instances this is fine but in others it is better to provide your own description, together with a selection of keywords which you can use to help index your own site.

To do this the META tag is used within the <HEAD> of each page you want registering with the engines, together with two important attributes; NAME and CONTENT.

The meta tags work in the following way:

```
<META NAME="description" CONTENT="Put a BRIEF
description of your site in here">

<META NAME="keywords" CONTENT="place, a, comma,
seperated, list, of, key, search, words, here">
```

And that's all there is to it.

How you choose to place this data within your site is entirely up to you. Whether you place it in every page or just the front page is a matter of personal choice. One thing is certain however. These meta statements must be present in any page whose URL has been submitted to the search engine if it is to have the desired effect.

Search engines to try:

Yahoo – http://www.yahoo.com

AltaVista – http://www.altavista.com

Excite – http://www.excite.co.uk

HotBot – http://www.hotbot.com

InfoSeek – http://www.infoseek.com

Lycos – http://www.lycos.com

UK Directory – http://www.ukdirectory.co.uk

UK Plus – http://www.ukplus.co.uk

Yellow Pages – http://www.yell.co.uk

Internet Directory UK – http://www.whatsnew.com/id/

And if you're looking for a site which will submit your details free to 20 of the world's biggest search engines visit:

http://www.submit-it.com

Newsgroups

Another way of gaining totally free publicity for your site is to advertise it in some of the thousands of Usenet newsgroups which exist.

These newsgroups act like electronic bulletin boards, each board being dedicated to a particular topic or subject. Users of the system can ask for help on particular topics, respond to the requests of others, or simply chat away to their heart's content in the hope somewone will respond.

The variation is astonishing with areas provided for just about anything you can think of, ranging from discussions about the TV science fiction series Star Trek through to business orientated groups, groups dedicated to the promotion of new websites and even some which are only available by subscription.

Because of the sheer number of these groups (estimates put it in excess of 20,000) a hierarchical structure has been imposed on the system and the groups have been collected under the following headings:

alt – Topics range from sex to cat health problems

bionet – Subjects of interest to biologists

bit – BITNET mailing lists

biz – Topics relating to business

clari – Clarinet groups direct from the UPI wire service

de – German groups

fr – French groups

k12 – Deals with education for the under-12s

comp – Computer topics

misc – A repository for things that don't fit elsewhere

news – All the latest on the Internet and more

rec – Topics for hobbyists of all descriptions

sci – Science-related topics

soc – Cultural and social topics

talk – Topics that lend themselves to debate

Usenet carries a massive amount of Internet data every day.

It's important to be discerning about the areas in which new site information is posted however, and care should be taken not to get too carried away and to post to every group you can find.

Such activities are frowned upon by the Internet community and are known as spams, for reasons which we won't go into here (actually it has something to do with the Monty Python sketch about the pork product of the same name).

In extreme cases spammers can find themselves having their Internet access accounts taken away by their service providers so if you do intend to publicise your site within the Usenet groups take care only to post into relevant subject areas – you have been warned!

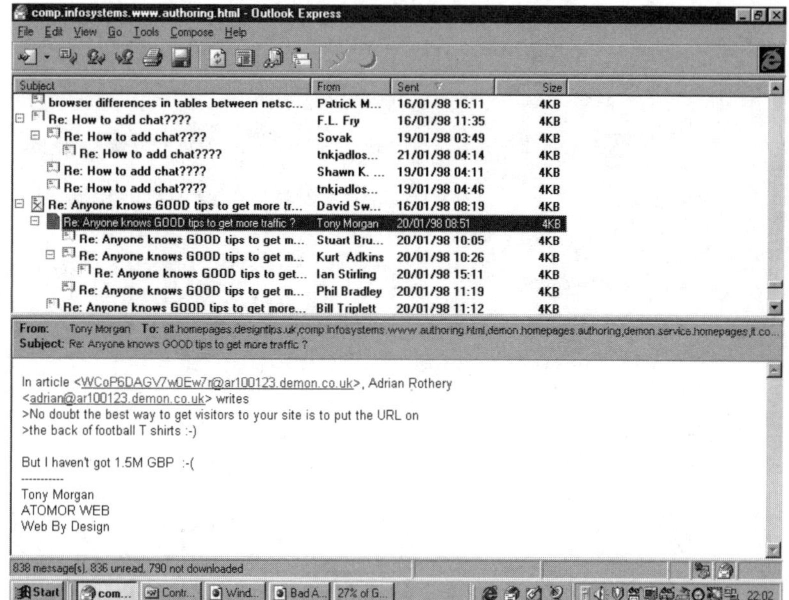

Banner Ads

For those wishing to promote business sites or private users with a little cash to hand, banner advertisements can be an extremely effective way of informing the Internet community of your work.

There are a great many sites on the web today that generate revenue by selling advertising space on their pages and getting your name onto their pages is a sure-fire way of attracting visitors to see your work.

Banner advertisements are graphic images which are submitted to a site for due display. Payment is usually gathered in one of two main ways – by click through or by impression.

A site which charges $300 for 10,000 click throughs, for example, will take the cash and display your advertisement until 10,000 people have seen your link and actually clicked on it to visit your pages.

A per impression rate may prove to be less effective as the cash paid will only give you, say, 10,000 appearances of your advert. It will not guarantee that the specified number of visitors will actually take the time to go to your site.

As with all advertising it pays to shop around to get the best deal for your money. Bear in mind however, that as with traditional advertisements the more popular the site you wish your ad to appear on the more it is likely to cost.

HANDY TIP

For a list of helpful advertising links visit: http://www.matrixpoint.com/advert.htm

Identifying high profile sites on which to advertise your own site is an art form in its own right and as the practice of advertising on the Web is still in its infancy it can be difficult to hit the right spots first time every time.

Search engines are always good places to start as they are used by millions of people each day and following that news and popular interest sites such as Ziff Davis (http://www.zdnet.com) or the Microsoft Network (http://www.msn.com).

Link Exchanges

Link exchanges are a great way to spread the word of your site. All that's required is that the designer create a banner ad similar to those used by the pay-per-advertisement sites.

Once the banner has been created it is simply a matter of registering with a suitable exchange service, for example http://www.linkexchange.com. The service will place your advertisement on the homepages of others who also belong to the scheme, in return all you have to do is place ads for their sites on yours. It may not be to everyone's taste but it can be a very convenient way to spread the word.

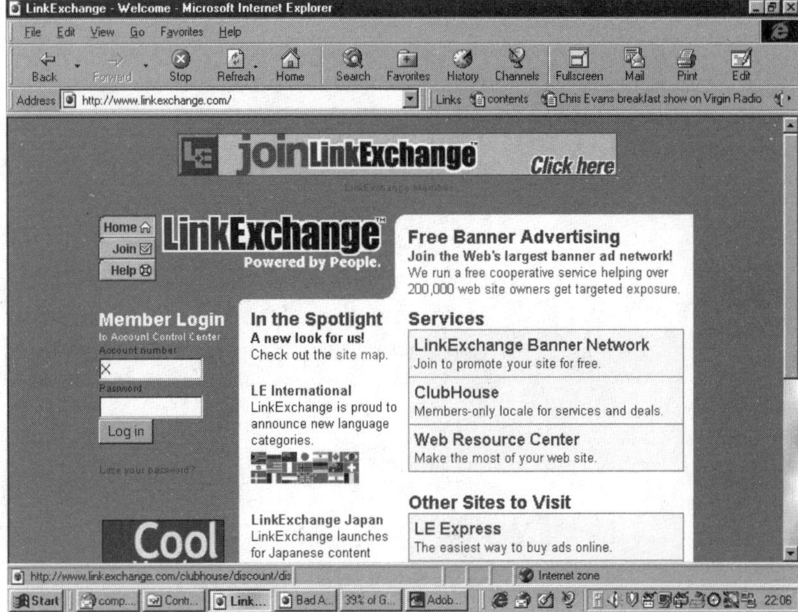

Other Methods

With link exchanges, newsgroups, ad banners and search engines dealt with, the major ways of advertising your web presence have already been covered.

There are, however, two other methods you might like to try.

The first is simple, effective and free! Delve deep into your email program and find the settings for the signature.

The signature is a piece of text you can create which is automatically appended to the bottom of every email you send out. Although it sounds very simple it does allow you to spread the word quickly and easily, the only drawback is that you will need to have a lot of friends and acquaintances to produce a significant increase in visits to your site.

Finally, why not try the traditional media. There are an ever growing number of print magazines dedicated to the world of the Internet, all of which regularly include pages of links to top sites the world over. Surf the web a little and look the publishers up. Drop them a line and see what happens. If you catch it right you can watch your popularity rocket.

Index

A

B

C

D

E

F

G

H

I

J

K

L

M

N

O

P

Q

R

S